LIGHT UP
—— *The* ——
DARKNESS

Breaking the Grip of Fear and Depression

MELODY R. FIELDS

©2025 by Melody R. Fields

Published by hope*books
2217 Matthews Township Pkwy
Suite D302
Matthews, NC 28105
www.hopebooks.com

hope*books is a division of hope*media

Printed in the United States of America

First paperback edition.
Paperback ISBN: 979-8-89185-247-1
Hardcover ISBN: 979-8-89185-248-8
Ebook ISBN: 979-8-89185-251-8
Library of Congress Number: 2025940537

Endorsements

"The book you are holding is full of practical, Biblical principles that will empower you to overcome whatever storms you may be facing. Through her own life experiences, Melody has learned that these principles work.

I have had the privilege of watching her walk through severe trials, to only come out better on the other side. While some allow the storm to break them, she has allowed it to draw her closer to Christ. Now, she stands in a position to help others navigate through their own troubles.

As you prayerfully read through this book and follow the steps outlined, God will do the same for you."

Doug Norman
Senior Pastor, Bridge of Hope Worship Center, Milan, IN

"If you've ever suffered from fear or depression, then you know how debilitating they can be. That's why I'm so thankful for my friend Melody and her willingness to share her journey with us.

In *Light Up the Darkness*, she opens up her life to bring hope through Jesus Christ to those who struggle daily. Not only will this book encourage those battling darkness, but it will also help others gain a deeper understanding of these challenges—some of which we may not even recognize in the people around us.

I encourage you to read, learn, and put into practice the blueprint Melody has shared."

Danny Wolford
Retired Pastor, First Christian Church, Greensburg, IN

"In *Light Up the Darkness*, Melody Fields offers a faith-driven approach to navigating the overwhelming emotions of depression, fear, and anxiety. Through her personal testimony and spiritual wisdom, she vulnerably highlights the transformative power of surrendering your burdens to God, embracing emotional honesty, and finding strength while connecting to faith. Melody serves as a guiding light for those seeking freedom from darkness by encouraging prayer, reflection, and unconditional support from a devoted community. With a focus on trusting in God & His promises, *Light Up the Darkness* presents tangible and effective tools for overcoming life's challenges— learning to pour from a full, rather than, an empty cup."

Ashley Pennington, M.A.
Mental Health Professional, Speaker, Blogger,
Author of *Love, Ashley P.*, and Podcast Host of *A Penny for
Your Thoughts: Lifting Shame & Building Community

A Word of Care Before You Begin

This book speaks openly about the realities of fear, depression, emotional pain, and spiritual exhaustion. While my heart is to offer hope and healing through Jesus, I also recognize that some parts of my story—and the reflection questions or prayer prompts—may stir up difficult emotions or memories.

If you find anything overwhelming, please give yourself permission to pause. Take a break. Talk with someone you trust. If you're in a place where you need additional support, don't hesitate to reach out—resources like the 988 Suicide & Crisis Lifeline are available 24/7.

This book isn't meant to replace counseling, medical treatment, or therapy—it's here to walk alongside you. One step at a time, one truth at a time.

You are not broken beyond repair. You are not alone. And you are deeply loved by a God who sees you, knows you, and walks with you—every step of the way.

"The Lord is close to the brokenhearted;

He rescues those whose spirits are crushed."

Psalm 34:18

Dedication

To the weary, the anxious, the brokenhearted—
If fear has gripped you, if depression has drained you,
Please know this: you are not alone.
Jesus sees, Jesus stays, and Jesus heals.

I pray these words lead you gently back to the
One who brings light to every shadow.

Table of Contents

Acknowledgments

First and foremost, I want to give all my thanks and praise to God. He is my everything, and I'm so grateful for His faithfulness and presence in every step of this journey. To God be the glory.

To my husband, Vernon—thank you for always believing in me. Your patience, support, and endless encouragement have meant the world to me throughout this writing process. Thank you for the quiet weekends that gave me the space to breathe, pray, and write. I love you more than words can say.

To my amazing kids, daughter-in-law, and all of my precious grandchildren—you are my heart. Your encouragement has been a gift I cherish more than words can say.

To my family and friends—your curiosity, excitement, and constant check-ins about the book truly touched my heart. Knowing you cared kept me accountable and inspired me to keep going

To those who came alongside me during the early stages of this book—thank you for your time, encouragement, and willingness to walk with me. Your presence, prayers, and thoughtful insights helped to strengthen the message and gave me the confidence to keep moving forward in obedience to what God was calling me to write.

I'm grateful to hope*books for publishing this work and helping bring it to life.

I truly can't say enough to express how thankful I am to everyone who in their own way played a part in making this book and dream happen. My deepest thanks to all.

Special Thanks

To Pastor Sue Thurston—thank you for your obedience and sensitivity to the Holy Spirit on a day that became a turning point in my healing journey. Though you were just visiting, your words spoke directly to my heart in a way only God could orchestrate. I'm grateful for your presence that day and your permission to share that experience in this book.

To Pastor Ben Bausback—thank you for allowing me to share the childhood story you once told about losing sight of your mom in the lazy river. That simple image stayed with me and brought clarity to something I couldn't quite name. I had already written the chapter, but it never felt complete—until I heard your story. It helped me recognize where I was at that point in my own journey: caught in the current of life, with my eyes off Jesus. But He had never left.

Thank you for your transparency, and for allowing me to include a moment that brought both insight and healing—not just to the chapter, but to my heart.

Preface

Before we begin, I want to share something from my heart. You may notice that some biblical and foundational truths come up more than once throughout these pages—and that's intentional. We live in a world filled with endless noise, constant demands, and a pace that rarely gives our hearts or minds time to rest. Healing doesn't usually happen just by hearing a truth once. Sometimes we need to hear the same hope again and again before it reaches the places that hurt the most.

My prayer is that each time you come across a familiar truth, it will settle a little deeper into your heart—allowing God's Word to gently peel back the layers of pain and reach areas you didn't even realize were still wounded.

I've been there. And I've learned that freedom doesn't come from pretending everything's fine or trying to push through in your own strength. It often begins by noticing the quiet lies that have slipped into our hearts—ones we didn't even realize we were starting to believe. They creep in slowly, twisting how we see ourselves, how we see God, and how we see our future. Over time, they rob us of peace and leave us feeling stuck.

But God's truth breaks even the deepest lies, and it's where real healing begins.

That's why I wrote this book. *Light Up the Darkness* was born from my own journey—through fear, through depression, and through a season of learning to trust God's truth more than the lies. I know what it's like to feel stuck in survival mode, unsure if things will ever really change. But I've also seen what happens when the smallest flicker of God's light breaks into the darkness. Things begin to shift. Shame loses its grip. Hope starts to rise again.

Introduction

This book is a mix of real-life stories, biblical truth, and practical tools that have helped me fight back when fear and depression felt overwhelming.

At the end of each chapter, you'll find a few healing steps and guided prayers. These are simple but intentional tools to help you process what you've read, reflect on God's truth, and talk to Him honestly about your own journey. There's no pressure—just space to be real, heal, and grow.

I'm not writing from a place of having it all figured out—I'm writing as someone who's been in the thick of it and has seen the faithfulness of God show up, again and again, with grace, strength, and light.

My hope and prayer is that these pages will help you see the battle more clearly—and help you recognize that you don't have to face it alone or unequipped. Together, we'll confront the things that have kept you stuck for too long. We'll talk honestly about shame, silence, spiritual warfare, and the lies that try to keep us in the dark. But we won't stop there. Because the light of Christ is stronger than any darkness, and His truth changes everything.

I want to be honest with you, though—this journey won't be instant or easy. Healing takes time, and it doesn't look the same for everyone. That's why I need to say this upfront: this isn't a quick fix, and it's not a replacement for professional help. If you're seeing a counselor, taking medication, or considering it—know that there is strength in getting support. This book is simply one more piece of the journey. It's a companion for the hard days, and a reminder that you're not crazy, not broken beyond repair, and definitely not alone.

I also pray that somewhere along the way, these pages might help you begin to recognize a few of the deeper roots—those places where fear or pain first crept in and started shaping how you see yourself, God, and the world around you. You don't have to untangle it all at once. Sometimes just seeing what's been buried is the first step toward freedom.

This isn't about pretending everything is fine. It's about learning how to fight with the right weapons, standing firm in God's promises, and stepping into the life He's called you to live. It won't always be easy—but it will be worth it.

Let's take this journey together.

"You light a lamp for me.
The Lord, my God, lights up my darkness."
Psalm 18:28

CHAPTER 1
Shadows Within: Understanding Depression

THE GRIPPING SENSATION

Depression often doesn't shout, it whispers. But sometimes, it crashes over you without warning. I remember feeling like the ground beneath me was shifting, like I was losing my hold on everything that once felt steady. The gripping sensation of *"I'm losing it! I'm really losing it!"* can hit out of nowhere, like a wave you never saw coming. It doesn't matter if it's the quiet of the night or the bright light of day—those thoughts swirl endlessly, leaving you restless, uneasy, and searching for answers you can't quite find.

Maybe the weight is something you can't even name, but it's there—an ache that settles into your chest, slowly draining your energy, your joy, and even your sense of who you are. You can't explain why, but it feels as if a part of you is disappearing. This is a scary place to be. No matter how much you try to push those feelings aside, they linger, clouding your mind and leaving you feeling more distant from peace than ever before. When the heaviness becomes a constant companion, it can start to feel like there's no way out. I understand that feeling, because I've walked through it too.

A Personal Struggle

In that season, it wasn't just fleeting doubts or moments of fear—it was a deep sadness that wrapped itself around me and refused to let go. There was a sense of insignificance that kept whispering, *You don't matter as much as you thought.* It was confusing. No matter how hard I tried to shake it, the sadness and unwanted feelings attached to me like a shadow.

I told myself, *Just keep pushing through.* I rationalized that if I stayed busy—if I kept checking tasks off on my never-ending to-do list—it would all eventually pass. Unknowingly, distraction became my survival strategy. But deep down, I knew something wasn't right. I was so tired. I looked fine on the outside, but inside, the cracks were growing—and I was getting too weary to keep pretending.

It didn't hit me all at once. It crept in quietly, steadily, like twilight stretching its fingers across the sky, gradual, unassuming. At first, it was just a faint heaviness, something I could dismiss as a passing mood or a temporary season. But over time, its grip tightened, like a slow-moving tide rising higher until I was submerged before I even realized I was drowning.

The world didn't change, but my ability to bear it did.

Friend, if any of this resonates with you, if you are barely holding on, suffocated by the weight of it all, please know: you are not alone. Before we go further, I'd love for you to pause and reflect on your journey.

Ask yourself:

- Have you lost interest in the things you used to enjoy?
- Do you struggle with indecisiveness?
- Are you more emotional than usual—or maybe more numb?
- Do you feel disconnected from those around you?
- Are you pushing yourself through each day behind a smile no one questions?
- Does the thought of starting a project feel overwhelming?
- Does exhaustion settle in not just physically, but emotionally and spiritually?
- Are you putting on a happy face that betrays your true feelings?

If you answered yes to several of these, you may be walking through a season of depression. But how do you explain what's wrong—when you're not even sure yourself?

Let's start here: Reaching out is not a weakness. It's courage and a step towards healing. Talk to a trusted friend or a godly mentor. And if you don't know where to turn, please call 988, the Suicide & Crisis Lifeline—available 24/7. Caring people are ready to listen and help.

Depression isn't just an emotional struggle—it can be a battle on multiple fronts, including the spiritual one. The Bible reminds us in Ephesians 6:12: "For we are not fighting against flesh-and-blood enemies, but against evil rulers and authorities of the unseen world, against mighty powers in this dark world, and against evil spirits in the heavenly places."

The National Institute of Mental Health (NIMH) defines depression as a state of mind that negatively affects how you think, feel, and act. It varies in intensity, and anyone can be susceptible to it at one time or another. It's more than just feeling "down." It can be a persistent weight, often triggered by unresolved trauma, emotional wounds, or life events that shake the foundation of our security.

When life changes—for good or bad—it brings stress to our minds and bodies. If these stressors remain unchecked, they can manifest into harmful emotional states such as depression, fear, or anxiety. Depression and fear rarely have just one cause; it tends to creep in through a mix of circumstances. Some are hidden and some not, but often it's not until we stop and look back that we begin to realize what we have been carrying.

Here are a few possible root causes to consider:

- **Loss & Grief:** The loss of a loved one, the end of a relationship, or job loss can deeply impact mental well-being. Even good things—like the birth of a baby or starting a new job—can stir up unexpected emotions. I've seen how the arrival of a newborn can fill a home with joy, but also bring a deep sense of overwhelm. That transition from independence to parenthood is beautiful, but it can also feel like you've lost pieces of the life you once knew. It's more common than we realize to grieve the freedom we had before, even while being grateful for the new season we're in.

- **Trauma:** Past or recent traumatic events, accidents, violence, or natural disasters can leave lasting emotional wounds.

- **Life Transitions:** Even positive changes, like a new job, moving, or welcoming a child, can add stress that triggers depression.

- **Substance Abuse:** The misuse of alcohol, drugs, or prescription medication can contribute to and worsen depression.

- **Chronic Pain or Illness:** Living with a prolonged medical condition can take both a physical and mental toll.

- **Financial Stress:** Worrying about money can weigh heavily on a person's mental state.

- **Fear & Anxiety:** Persistent fear can be a major driver of depression, particularly when it leads to a sense of helplessness.

- **Feeling Out of Control:** When circumstances feel beyond our control, hopelessness can take root.

- **A Sense of Failure:** Constantly feeling like you're falling short can create a cycle of self-doubt and despair.

Recognizing the root is the first step toward healing. Depression thrives in silence but the light begins to break its grip.

THE DANGER OF SURVIVAL MODE

I can see it so clearly now—I was stuck in survival mode. My days were packed with ministry, family, and work responsibilities. Every hour had something to do, someone to help, or a task that couldn't wait. On the outside, it looked like I was handling it all. But on the inside, I was unraveling.

I didn't realize it at the time, but little by little, I began to believe the lie that staying busy would fix what was broken inside. I thought if I just kept moving, kept doing, everything would eventually settle down. I thought productivity would silence the ache in my soul. But in reality, the very things I thought were helping me were actually draining me. I had replaced stillness with striving, rest with rushing, and time with God with constant activity.

I still went through the motions—I went to church, served, showed up where I was needed. But there's a difference between showing up and being filled up. I was giving out without being replenished. And to serve God the way He desires—with my heart and joy—I needed Him to refill me. I needed His presence, not just more pressure. I didn't see how empty I had become. I was pouring myself out for everyone else but never stopping to be refilled. I thought slowing down would bring relief. I imagined peace would flood in the moment I paused—like cool water washing over dry ground. But when I finally did slow down, it wasn't peaceful. It was overwhelming. All the sadness, fear, and disconnection I had been pushing down came rushing to the surface. It hit like a tidal wave—unprocessed grief, hidden anxieties, the quiet ache of exhaustion I had ignored for far too long. I had spent so long trying to be strong, trying to carry the weight on my own, that I didn't know how to simply be still with God anymore.

That moment was the beginning for me. I couldn't outrun the pain or numb it with activity. I had to face it. And more importantly, I had to return to the One who never stopped waiting for me. Because true rest—lasting, healing rest—was never going to be found in doing more. It could only be found in drawing close to Jesus.

I'm reminded of the story of Elijah in 1 Kings 19. After one of the most powerful moments in his ministry, calling down fire from heaven—he ran. Exhausted and afraid, he collapsed under a tree and told God he wanted to die. He was burnt out, overwhelmed, and completely done. And how did God respond? He didn't shame him or tell him to pull it together. He let him rest. He sent an angel to care for him. And when Elijah was ready, God spoke— not through wind, or fire, or earthquake—but through a gentle whisper.

That whisper reminds me that God meets us in the quiet. He waits until we stop running. And when we do, He gently speaks the words we need most—not with condemnation but with kindness.

Scripture says in Isaiah 30:15, "Only in returning to me and resting in me will you be saved. In quietness and confidence is your strength." But the truth is, I had been doing the opposite—rushing instead of resting in His sweet presence. It took coming to the end of myself to realize that God never asked me to carry it all. He just asked me to come. And as I started to slow down and listen, I began to realize something wasn't right. I still hadn't fully grasped the depth of what was going on inside me, but I could feel the weight of it building. There was more beneath the surface than I had allowed myself to face.

THE BURDEN BALLOON

That's when God gently gave me a picture—I call it the Burden Balloon. Picture it as a simple symbol of daily surrender—something God gives us to help us release what we were never meant to carry alone. Imagine that each day, you're handed a floating balloon to fill with your daily burdens to release to God. As the hours pass, you begin filling it with your fears, stress, and worries. A negative thought here. An anxious moment there. A conversation that left you rattled. A responsibility you're not sure how to carry. Each unreleased burden adds a little more weight, stretching the balloon a bit further. What started as something light and manageable begins to feel strained, like it can burst at any moment.

It wasn't meant to be that way. The balloon was never designed to carry the pressure of everything you're trying to hold together. It was meant to be released—lifted into God's loving hands, where the weight isn't yours to bear alone. But here's where the problem begins: we tend to hold on. We carry our worries from one day into the next, letting them accumulate silently.

We gather our concerns, but we don't release them. And over time, what started as a simple balloon becomes unbearably heavy.

The emotional strain becomes physical. The spiritual weight becomes personal. We try to manage it, but eventually, we feel like we're about to pop.

God didn't design us to carry that kind of load. He doesn't expect us to walk through life pretending we're fine while we're slowly being crushed inside. He invites us to hand it over—not just once but daily. Over and over again, before the pressure becomes more than we were ever meant to hold.

And here's the beautiful truth: you don't have to carry that weight anymore. God never intended for you to hold on to the burdens of depression, fear, anxiety, or emotional exhaustion. He never meant for your balloon to sag under the strain of life. Instead, He gently invites you—again and again—to release it to Him.

"Give your burdens to the Lord, and he will take care of you. He will not permit the godly to slip and fall." (Psalm 55:22)

God doesn't just ask us to give Him our burdens—He promises to carry them. Scripture reminds us in Psalm 68:19, "Praise the Lord; praise God our savior! For each day he carries us in his arms."

That's what it feels like when God comes alongside to lift what's too heavy for you. The burden may not be gone, but it's no longer crushing. The concern might still exist, but the heaviness lifts when you place it in His hands. It's no longer all-consuming because you've chosen to trust the One who is strong enough to carry it—and faithful enough to carry you through it.

A Path To Letting Go

Take a moment to reflect on your own balloon. What fears or burdens have slowly filled the space in your heart? What have you been carrying that's quietly been weighing you down? Maybe you've been holding so much for so long that the idea of slowing down feels terrifying—almost impossible. Holding it all together has become second nature, and the thought of letting go, even for a moment, might feel like everything could unravel.

I found out early in this journey that healing is far from a one-time moment—it's a process. Sometimes it's slow, sometimes it's messy, and often, it has to be repeated. But that doesn't mean it's not working. It just means you're human, and thankfully, God is patient. Letting go can feel risky, especially when holding on is how you've coped, survived, or stayed strong for everyone else. But what if letting go isn't the end of control—it's the beginning of real peace?

Here's a truth I've learned: healing begins by slowing down. When we pause long enough to breathe, we create space for God to meet us—right in the middle of the mess. It's not easy. It might feel unfamiliar, even overwhelming. But that's exactly where real healing begins.

Fear thrives in the dark. It grows louder in silence. But the moment we name our burdens before God and place them in His hands, their grip on us begins to break. The enemy loses power when we stop hiding and start surrendering. Healing unfolds over time. Some days, I had to hand my worries back to God again and again. And that's okay. He never grows tired of our surrender. He welcomes it every single time.

Because surrender isn't weakness—it's strength in action. It's choosing, again and again, to say, "God, I can't carry this alone. I need You." It's not a one-time decision. It's a daily rhythm. A faithful habit that slowly strengthens your heart. It didn't happen overnight for me, but over time, God gently taught me: the more often I let go, the more peace I found. Over time, I realized that releasing the balloon wasn't about removing every worry—it was about shifting the weight into hands much stronger than mine.

So take a deep breath, my friend. Unclench your fists, open your hands, and let the balloon go. The concern may still be there—but the weight no longer has to be. Because when you release it, you'll find that God is ready to catch it—every single time.

HEALING STEPS:

1. **Pause and Reflect.** Take a few moments to name what you're feeling as best you can. What emotions are weighing heaviest on your heart? Writing them down can help untangle the negative or messy feelings and bring clarity.

   _____

   _____

   _____

   _____

   _____

   _____

   _____

2. **Bring It to God.** Pray intentionally, asking Him to take each burden from you. Be specific. Share what's on your heart, no matter how messy, big or small it feels.

   _____

   _____

   _____

   _____

   _____

   _____

   _____

3. **Practice Daily Surrender.** Like the "Burden Balloon," releasing your worries is a daily practice. Some days, you might need to do it multiple times, and that's okay. God is patient, and He never grows tired of carrying your burdens. List your specific worries below.

_____

_____

_____

_____

_____

_____

_____

4. **Find Support.** Reach out to someone you trust—a friend, mentor, or Christian counselor. You don't have to navigate this alone.

Healing isn't about getting everything right; it's about letting God meet you in the middle of the mess. Even small steps of surrender open the door for His light to break through. You're already farther along than you realize, just by choosing to keep walking.

SCRIPTURES

Pray these verses out loud during your quiet time. Speaking God's Word has power, and it will help solidify the truth of His promises in your heart, mind, and spirit:

- "Don't worry about anything; instead, pray about everything. Tell God what you need, and thank Him for all He has done. Then you will experience God's peace, which exceeds anything we can understand. His peace will guard your hearts and minds as you live in Christ Jesus." Philippians 4:6-7

- "Cast your burden upon the Lord and He will sustain you; He will never allow the righteous to be shaken." Psalm 55:22 NASB

- "When I am afraid, I will put my trust in You." Psalm 56:3 NASB

- "Come to me, all of you who are weary and carry heavy burdens, and I will give you rest." Matthew 11:28

PRAYER PROMPT

Lord. Forgive me for taking my eyes off of You. Forgive me for my focus being on everything else but You. Lord, Open my eyes to see what You see. I pray for Your strength, clarity and wisdom as we deal with these emotions head on, together. Help me to be honest with myself and to You during this process of healing. Lord, open my heart to see how You see me. Help me to grab hold of the truth of being a child of the most High King and that I'm loved and You sing over me. I'm worthy by the saving grace of Jesus.

Lord, I need your help to daily release my burdens to You. When I pick up my troubles and dwell on the negative thoughts and feelings that pull me down, replace them with wholesome thoughts of who You are. Remind me of Your goodness and willingness to be my shelter, refuge, and strength.

Thank you Lord for Your faithfulness. Let the words that "I'm an overcomer through Christ" be present in my mind and heart when I struggle. Romans 8:37 NIV says, "No, in all these things we are more than conquerors through Him who loved us." Thank you, Lord.

In Jesus' name I pray,

Amen.

CHAPTER 2

How Our History Can Shape Our Fears

FEAR, FAITH, AND THE MUD PIT

A few years ago, I signed up for an endurance race—a challenge filled with messy obstacles that tested more than just physical strength. It pushed me out of my comfort zone and revealed fears I didn't even realize were still there. What I thought would be a physical challenge turned into something much deeper.

About halfway through my first race, my teammates and I reached a mud pit. The water, thick with debris, rose just above my chest, swirling in murky chaos. At the center stood a towering wall—wide, slick with grime, and heavy with intimidation. I froze.

Before I could fully process what was happening, panic gripped me. My heart pounded, and my breath caught in my throat. I stood frozen, unable to move. There was no way I was going under that wall and into the muddy water beneath it. I felt trapped in a moment that suddenly seemed bigger than me.

It was like fear had been lying in wait—quiet and hidden, like a lion crouching low, ready to pounce. And in that vulnerable moment, it sprang up fast and fierce. I didn't see it coming, and I didn't know how to stop it.

Rationally, I knew I was safe. I had watched several people complete the task before me. I knew hundreds had done it before now. But fear doesn't follow logic. It doesn't respond to facts. It thrives in the unseen places—where reason can't reach and where emotions run deep. Even when everything around you seems fine, fear can rise up out of nowhere—fast, fierce, and paralyzing.

One of my teammates noticed the panic in my wide, tear-filled eyes. She came over, placed a steady hand on my shoulder, and spoke softly: "It's okay. I'll go first. You can follow me. I will reach under, grab your hand, and pull you through." Her calm voice felt like a lifeline in the chaos of my thoughts. Step by step, with steady patience, she guided me under the wall and through. That moment wasn't just about completing an obstacle—it was about facing fear and refusing to let it win.

Looking back now, I realize that fear didn't begin that day in the mud pit. It had been planted long before, quietly, almost unnoticed. I hadn't fully realized it was a broken part of me— one that lay hidden beneath the surface, waiting for moments of vulnerability to rise again. That quiet fear would later resurface in ways I never expected—especially when it came to protecting the ones I loved most.

But what happened in the mud wasn't the start—it was the stirring. The broken part of me didn't begin at that moment. It had been forming quietly over time, shaped by earlier experiences that left me feeling vulnerable and exposed. One of those moments happened years before— in a river, on what seemed like an ordinary summer afternoon.

The River Depths

When I was a teenager, my boyfriend (now husband) Vernon, and I decided to go tubing on a nearby river one summer afternoon. The sun was shining brightly, the water was cool and inviting, and the day seemed perfect. Most of the river was shallow and calm, and we floated along lazily, soaking in the moment.

Drifting along, we came to a deeper section of the river where a rope swing dangled from a tree on the bank. Vernon, who had grown up swimming in rivers, was thrilled. *"I've got to try that swing!"* he said, already making his way to the bank.

I, however, was perfectly content to stay on my warm tube, watching him as he went. But as he headed toward the swing, I didn't really think it through—I just knew I didn't want to be the one sitting out. So I slid off my tube and waded into the water.

At first, everything felt fine. The water was calm and steady, but as I ventured farther from the safety of my tube, everything quickly changed. A cool current grabbed at my legs, pulling me off balance. Before I could react, I was underwater.

The world around me shifted, tilting in ways that made no sense. I couldn't tell which way was up. Water rushed into my nose and ears, and panic squeezed the air from my lungs. I flailed, desperate for a breath, but the current was stronger than me. I felt helpless, powerless against the force pulling me under.

Just as I thought I couldn't hold my breath any longer, a strong hand broke through the water and grabbed my arm. Vernon. He pulled me out of the current and back to the surface, holding me steady as I gasped for air. I clung to him, my chest heaving and my heart pounding, shaking at the thought of how close I had come to disaster.

That day left a lasting impression on me when it came to water. But it wasn't just the river I feared. It was the helplessness that settled in—and the realization that some things are simply beyond me.

THE IMPRINT OF LOSS

But the river wasn't the only thing that stayed with me. Some moments in life carve deep grooves into our hearts that can never be erased. For me, the deepest cut came from a loss that changed everything.

When I was a young teenager, my older brother passed away suddenly. His death was like a lightning bolt—unexpected, devastating, and impossible to process. One moment, he was there, full of life and laughter, and the next, he was gone.

Grief swept through our family like a tidal wave, pulling us under and leaving us gasping for air. We were together, but we weren't really together. It felt like we were all sealed inside a delicate glass bubble—so thin, so stretched by sorrow, even one word could cause it to shatter and take us with it. We were close enough to see each other, but we couldn't reach one another. None of us wanted to be the one to break the silence—for fear it would unleash a flood of emotion we weren't ready to face.

In that silence, regret started to echo in my own heart. Loss can be harsh. It often brings a measure of regret, and this time was no different. Regret raged through my thoughts: *"I should've spent more time with him. I wish I had told him I loved him more often."* But death is cruel in the way it steals not just life, but the chance to go back and fix the things that once seemed small but now are of great importance.

My parents, weighed down by their own deep heartbreak, seemed distant. At fourteen, I was carrying my own grief, trying to make sense of a world that no longer felt whole. My little sister, once so full of energy, withdrew when she was at home. But outside, she reached for her friends, clinging to connection in her own way.

We all coped the best we could, alone. It reshaped each one of us. We were walking a path we didn't want to take, but there was no turning back.

I remember that most days, I didn't even want to come home from school. Not because I didn't love my family or know they loved me—but because everything had changed. The magnitude of our loss hung heavy in our home. We were shells of ourselves, moving through the same house, but no longer living in it.

I grasped at sports and clung to friends like a lifeline—anything to keep me from facing the emptiness that waited at home. I threw myself into the normalcy of practices, games, and conversations that weren't wrapped in grief, because at home, everything reminded me that he was gone.

I didn't fully understand it at the time, but it was as if death and grief had mugged me—stealing my brother, and with him, any sense of peace I once had—leaving behind a heavy heart full of what ifs. For the first time, I understood how fragile life really was—how someone could be here one moment and gone the next. And with that realization, it felt like everything that had once been "normal" was gone too.

I went from being a carefree young girl to someone who quietly carried the weight of *what if?*

What if I couldn't protect the people I loved?

What if I couldn't protect the people I loved?

What if I ever lost my child?

And although I knew God then, I couldn't help but wonder how He allowed this to happen.

TRADING FEAR FOR TRUST

In those early years, fear showed up quietly in flashes, in overthinking, in sleepless nights. But years later, when I became a mom, I thought I had handled my grief. That's when the *what ifs* became more frequent. That's when I realized—my fear hadn't gone away. It had simply moved. What began as the ache of losing my brother had quietly shifted into the fear of losing my own children. These thoughts weren't loud or obvious. They slipped in quietly, weaving themselves into everyday moments, until I hardly noticed how tightly they were gripping me.

Surprisingly, it wasn't the toddler years that brought the deepest fear. It was when they started pulling away—when they gained independence and stepped beyond the circle of my protection.

When they started driving.

When they went out with friends.

When they were making choices I couldn't help guide them.

It was my loss that first gave fear a place to grow—a seed that took root quietly, never once confronted. I carried the weight of old wounds, shaped by heartbreak I couldn't let go of. Without realizing it, that weight colored how I saw the world and how I parented.

Back then, I didn't recognize what was happening. I just felt the fear. Over time, I began to see that my anxiety and fear weren't really about their driving, their friendships, or their independence. It was about loss. It was about protection. It was about control.

I had spent so much time trying to hold on, to prevent the worst from happening, when in reality, I was never truly in control to begin with. *Only God was.*

THE BATTLE BETWEEN FEAR AND LETTING GO

One of the most surprising things I've learned about fear is that it doesn't always look like fear. It doesn't always show up as panic or dread. Sometimes, it looks smart. Responsible. It disguises itself as wisdom and shows up in your thoughts like a helpful friend. It tells you that worrying is part of loving, that overthinking is just being prepared. And the sneakiest part? Fear whispers, "Just hold on a little tighter." It pretends to be protective—but really, it's about control. And the tighter we grip, the more fear takes over. It grows until our thoughts are crowded and our peace is nowhere to be found.

As a parent, I've come to understand that I was called to love, to guide, to protect in the ways I could—but never to carry what only God can hold. Still, I sometimes forget. I find myself gripping outcomes and trying to manage what was never mine to control. I get caught up in the *what ifs* and lose sight of the truth I know: their lives are not in my hands. They never were. Their future has always belonged to Him.

Letting go isn't a one-time choice—it's something I come back to again and again. Not with ease, but with faith. I return with open hands, trading the heaviness of anxiety for the quiet trust that God sees more than I ever could. Letting go doesn't mean I stop caring—it means I stop carrying what was never mine.

WHEN FEAR GROWS QUIETLY

There was a time when I lived in constant preparation mode. My mind would scan every situation, always searching for what could go wrong. I thought that made me a good parent—alert, careful, attentive. I told myself that being ready for anything was part of my job. But over time, that kind of mental planning wore me down. It took a toll. It started to drain my energy and joy, little by little.

But here's the part I need to be honest about: I didn't miss the sweetness of their childhood—I soaked it in. I was present for so much of it. The bedtime stories, the early morning giggles, the messy crafts at the kitchen table. I laughed. I listened. I lived it. The fear wasn't front and center back then. It was quiet. Dormant. Like something resting in the background. I didn't feel overwhelmed—I felt grateful.

It wasn't until life began to change that fear found a louder voice. As they got older, more independent, and the safety rails started to disappear, the fear stirred. A combination of life transitions, personal changes, and the natural loosening that comes with time created a perfect storm. That old fear, the one I thought I had outgrown, rose back up. Not suddenly, but steadily—like a tide that crept in quietly and began to shape my thinking in new ways. And the risks started to change. Scraped knees and playground mishaps became harder things—decisions that might carry lasting consequences, pain I couldn't predict or prevent. A wrong turn, a missed opportunity, an unexpected heartbreak—all of it felt heavier than anything I'd prepared for.

What made it harder was knowing I couldn't step in the way I used to. When they were small, I could intervene. I could comfort, redirect, protect. But now, those safety nets were gone. I had to let them choose for themselves—and sometimes stumble. Through the years I encouraged their independence and clapped at their milestones, something quiet tugged at me underneath: the constant, low hum of *what if?* It was a strange kind of tension. I believed in them, but I also knew the world wasn't always kind. That awareness settled in the background like a quiet, watchful presence.

FACING THE REAL FEAR

Eventually, I had to admit something deeper. The fear wasn't just about them. It was about me. About my past. About what

I'd lost. About the pain I'd felt as a teenager when I learned just how fragile life could be. I had told myself that if I could stay ahead of every possibility, maybe I could keep my children from experiencing that same pain—or keep myself from having to watch it.

That unhealed fear, the one I thought I'd buried, had grown into something heavy. Something that started to control my parenting, my prayers, and my peace. I was fiercely trying to protect them—but I was also, without realizing it, trying to protect myself. My heart had already broken once, and I was terrified of feeling that pain again. I wasn't just trying to keep them safe—I was trying to protect my heart from breaking.

And here's what I've come to learn: fear like that can't be managed. It has to be released. That's not always easy. Trusting God doesn't come without wrestling. There were days I whispered prayers through clenched hands:

"God, they are Yours. Help me trust You with them."

And I meant it. Not because I felt brave, but because I felt spent. I knew I couldn't carry this anymore. I wasn't created to.

The Truth About Suppressed Fear

For many years, I believed I had moved past my fears. That I'd matured. That faith had canceled them out. But the truth? I hadn't healed—I'd just buried them deeper. I wasn't walking in peace. I was walking in pressure.

Fear doesn't disappear when we ignore it. It waits. It influences the way we parent, the way we think, the way we react. It changes how we view the world and ourselves. Over time, it becomes a weight that wears us down from the inside out. I've come to see fear like an untreated wound. At first, you think it's nothing. You move on. But without care, it gets infected. It becomes something more serious. And eventually, it demands attention. Healing fear isn't about pretending it's not there. It's about noticing it, naming it, and letting God meet you in it. Not with shame—but with compassion. With patience. With hope.

HE MEETS US IN THE MESS

There was a moment when I was stuck in a mud pit during a race. I froze, overwhelmed by fear. My teammate could've run ahead. But she didn't. She stayed. She reached for me and walked me through it. That picture has stayed with me. Because that's how God is. He doesn't wait for us to be brave. He doesn't expect us to carry it all or get it all right before He shows up. He steps into the hard places, the stuck places, the places we're ashamed to admit we're still struggling. That's the God I've come to know—not one who waits for me to "figure it out," but one who comes close in the fear, in the silence, and in the mess.

And when I need reminding, this is the truth I hold onto:

"When you go through deep waters, I will be with you. When you go through rivers of difficulty, you will not drown. Whenyouwalkthroughthefireofoppression,youwillnotbeburnedup; the flames will not consume you" (Isaiah 43:2, NLT).

That verse isn't just poetry to me. It's a promise. It's a steady hand holding me up when I feel like I'm sinking. It's the reason I can keep letting go—even when fear tries to rise again.

Letting go certainly isn't something I've mastered. But I return to it one surrender at a time. And every time I do, I find the same faithful truth waiting for me: they were never mine to hold—and I was never alone in letting go.

HEALING STEPS

Healing begins when we stop avoiding our fears and start confronting them with God's strength. Here's what I've learned about facing fear with Him:

1. **Be Honest.** Take time to name your fears. Write them down, speak them out loud, and pray through them. Acknowledge what's weighing on your heart.

_____

_____

_____

_____

_____

_____

_____

2. **Take Inventory.** Reflect on your past experiences, relationships, and thoughts. What fears have shaped you?

_____

_____

_____

_____

_____

_____

_____

3. **Surrender Daily.** Release your fears to God, trusting Him to carry the weight you were never meant to bear. This isn't a one-time act; it's a daily practice of letting go and trusting Him.

_____

_____

_____

_____

_____

_____

_____

Friend, your struggles don't define you. God's word does. No matter how overwhelming they feel, you are not alone. God sees you. He loves you. He walks with you every step of the way.

Trust Him to carry the weight you've been holding onto. Let Him write a new chapter in your story, one filled with hope, healing, and peace.

SCRIPTURES

- "With a strong hand, and with an outstretched arm, For His mercy endures forever." Psalm 136:12 (NKJV)

- "Don't be afraid, for I am with you. Don't be discouraged, for I am your God. I will strengthen you and help you. I will hold you up with my victorious right hand." Isaiah 41:10

- "So be strong and courageous! Do not be afraid and do not panic before them. For the Lord your God will personally go ahead of you. He will neither fail you nor abandon you." Deuteronomy 31:6

PRAYER PROMPT

Dear Lord,

I thank You for showing me the fears that I have buried. God, I pray that You open my eyes to see the fears clearly so that we can deal with and heal from them together. I thank You for Your outstretched arm that is reaching for me even now. Lord, give me the courage and strength I need to face these fears. I'm asking for Your help and healing from these thoughts that can at times paralyze me.

I pray to embrace the full joy and beauty of this life You have blessed me with. I apply the blood of Jesus to my mind, body, and heart. I speak with the authority You have given me through Your sacrifice and through Your Word. I give my fears over to You, Lord. Help me not to take them back. Help me to trust You completely in all things. Deuteronomy 5:15 (NKJV) says, "The Lord your God brought You out from there by a mighty hand and by an outstretched arm" and I know You will do the same for me.

Thank You, Lord.

In Jesus' name I pray,

Amen.

CHAPTER 3
Invisible Chains

INVITING GOD ON THE JOURNEY

Before we begin this chapter, I want us to take a moment to pause, breathe, and invite God into this space. The things we're about to explore—things like fear, control, or the buried struggles we don't always recognize—can feel intimidating and uncomfortable. But you don't have to walk through this alone. God is already here, ready to bring clarity, healing, and freedom. He's not afraid of what's hidden. He's not overwhelmed by what's tangled.

God isn't asking you to figure it all out—only to be willing to take an honest look at what may be holding you back.

PRAYER

Heavenly Father,

I come to You with a heart full of gratitude, knowing that You are already working in my life. Thank You for the many blessings

You have given me—the air I breathe, the beauty of Your creation, and the grace that renews me each day. Lamentations 3:23 reminds me, "Great is His faithfulness; His mercies begin afresh each morning." And Lord, today, I need those fresh mercies.

I bring before You my struggles, my doubts, and the burdens I have carried for far too long. I ask for Your forgiveness where I have held onto fear instead of faith, control instead of trust, and unforgiveness instead of grace. Lord, I know there are areas in my life where I am still bound by invisible chains—chains I may not even fully recognize yet. Holy Spirit, open my eyes, revealing the places where I need healing and freedom.

Your Word in Isaiah 41:10 gives me hope: "Don't be afraid, for I am with you. Don't be discouraged, for I am your God. I will strengthen you and help you." Father, I am leaning on this promise today. I ask for the strength to face my buried wounds I have avoided, the courage to confront the emotions I have suppressed, and the wisdom to walk in the healing You are offering me.

Holy Spirit, shine Your light into the dark places of my heart. Replace fear with faith, doubt with trust, and pain with peace. Help me to see the lies I have believed and replace them with the truth of Your Word. Give me the confidence to surrender the things I have been trying to control, knowing that You are far more capable than I am.

I surrender this journey to You, Lord. I trust that as I take each step, You will guide me, heal me, and lead me into the fullness of life You have prepared for me.

In the precious name of Jesus,

Amen.

THE FEAR THAT HELD ME CAPTIVE

I've previously shared my greatest personal struggle with the invisible chain that kept me bound. This fear didn't appear out of nowhere. It was planted in my childhood, deeply rooted in the heartbreak of losing my brother.

That loss changed me. It wasn't just a moment of grief—it was a defining moment that altered how I saw the world. It forced me to confront a painful truth far too soon: no one is untouchable.

For many young people, there's a natural innocence that allows them to live freely—a quiet assurance that tomorrow will come, that the people they love will always be there. Tragedy feels like something distant, something that happens to other people. But for me, that belief shattered far too early.

At the time, I didn't realize it, but that fear became the lens through which I saw the world. It was like an unseen filter over my life, affecting the way I made decisions, approached relationships, and even experienced joy. I had unknowingly convinced myself that if I could just control enough things—plan enough, work at it enough, protect enough—I could somehow prevent pain from touching me or the people I loved.

Maybe you've felt that too. Maybe, like me, fear taught you to grip tighter instead of trusting deeper. Have you ever found yourself trying to manage the fear by managing everything around you—your life, your people, your outcomes?

HOW FEAR BECAME A WALL

When I look back on those years, I can now see how that fear took root in my life, growing like tangled vines around my heart and mind. It crept into my choices, held me back from stepping into new opportunities, and slowly stole the joy and freedom that God intended for me.

I was so afraid of losing someone, that I built walls around my heart, hoping they would keep me safe. I thought if I kept a tight enough grip on the people I loved, if I controlled my circumstances enough, I could prevent pain. But in reality, those walls didn't protect me—they trapped me, keeping me from fully embracing the life God had for me.

I can see now, that deep down, I wasn't fully trusting God—with my heart, my life, or even my loved ones. I clung to control, convinced it would shield me from the pain. But in the end, control didn't take the pain away. It didn't bring peace. It only kept me from truly living and left my heart unhealed.

An Open Door for the Enemy

And this, my friend, is exactly where the enemy found his opening.

Fear became the foothold he used to weave his way into my life. He didn't create the fear—it was already there—but he exploited it, twisting it into a weapon.

Over time, fear began shaping my thoughts, emotions, and decisions in ways I didn't always recognize. It wasn't just the joy of my adulthood that the enemy targeted—he reached for everything. My peace. My hope. Even my sense of purpose.

His goal was clear: to distort, diminish, and destroy whatever he could.

Some of you may feel this battle right now. Maybe you already know what your own invisible chain is—the thing that holds you back and weighs you down. Maybe it's fear, like mine. Or perhaps it's something else—shame, unforgiveness, guilt, or an old wound you've carried for far too long.

For some, that chain is easy to name. For others, it's harder to define, more like a quiet weight pressing down, a heaviness that lingers in the background of your life. Maybe you can't quite put it into words, but you feel it, a barrier that keeps you from fully stepping into the joy and freedom your heart longs for.

Wherever you find yourself in this journey, hear this: There is hope.

You are not alone. You don't have to carry this burden forever. Freedom is possible, one step at a time.

What's Holding You Back?

Now that we've invited God into this journey, I want to gently encourage you: you are safe here. There's no rush, no pressure—only an invitation to bring your burdens into the light. Take a deep breath and ask yourself:

- What has been holding me back?

- Is there a fear that keeps surfacing no matter how much I try to push it away?

- Are there wounds from the past still shaping how I see myself today?

- Have I been holding onto control, believing it would keep me safe?

- What is weighing down my heart, making it hard to move forward?

If you don't know the answer right away, that's okay. Healing begins with awareness. Sometimes, it takes time for clarity to come, and that's part of the process. God isn't in a hurry—He is patient, gentle, and walking with you every step of the way.

MOVING TOWARD FREEDOM

Recognizing our peace robbers is the first step, but true freedom comes when we actively surrender them to God. Letting go isn't always easy—it's a process, a daily decision to place our worries into His hands instead of carrying them alone.

Maybe surrender feels hard because peace has felt just out of reach for so long. Maybe control feels safer because uncertainty is uncomfortable. But the peace you long for is already yours in Christ. He never intended for you to carry these burdens alone.

That's why I remind myself of the Burden Balloon, I previously mentioned. Every worry, fear, or doubt is like a balloon I'm gripping tightly in my hands. The longer I hold on, the heavier it feels. But when I release it to God, it rises, lighter with every prayer, freer with every breath.

Each time you let go, you're stepping into the healing that Jesus has already won for you.

HEALING STEPS

RELEASING AND RECEIVING PEACE

Here are some steps that have helped me let go and embrace God's peace:

1. **Name Your Peace Robbers.**

   _____

   _____

   _____

   _____

   _____

_____

_____

2. **Write down the worries, fears, or doubts you've been carrying**. Identifying them brings them into the light.

_____

_____

_____

_____

_____

_____

3. **Release Them To God.** Picture yourself opening your hands and releasing your Burden Balloon to Him. Pray over each burden and trust that He is in control.

_____

_____

_____

_____

_____

_____

4. **Replace Worry with God's Truth.** Fill your heart with His promises through Scripture, worship, and prayer. When anxious thoughts come, counter them with His Word.

_____

_____

_____

_____

_____

_____

5. **Rest in His Presence Daily.** Peace isn't a one-time decision—it's a daily practice of surrendering and trusting. Spend time with God, even if it's just a few quiet moments in His presence. Write below any thoughts about your time with Him.

_____

_____

_____

_____

_____

_____

You don't have to carry the weight of your burdens alone. Each time fear creeps in, each time worry tightens its grip, picture yourself releasing your Burden Balloon. Whisper a prayer, open your hands, and trust that God is holding you.

He is faithful to meet you in your surrender and fill you with the peace you've longed for. No matter what yesterday looked like, today is a new opportunity to release, trust, and live in the peace He has already given you.

SCRIPTURES

- "Then you will know the truth, and the truth will set you free." John 8:32 (NIV)

- "Whatever is true, whatever is noble ... think about such things." Philippians 4:8 (NIV)

- "The Lord gives strength to His people; the Lord blesses His people with peace." Psalm 29:11 (NIV)

- "You will keep in perfect peace those whose minds are steadfast, because they trust in you." Isaiah 26:3 (NIV)

- "Cast all your anxiety on Him because He cares for you." 1 Peter 5:7 (NIV)

PRAYER PROMPT

Heavenly Father,

Thank You for always being faithful, for loving me unconditionally, and for never letting go of me (1 John 3:11). Lord, open my eyes and my heart to see what I have hidden from myself—the burdens, the fears, and the wounds I've carried far too long. Show me the places where I need healing, and help me to face them with Your strength rather than my own. Forgive me for the times I have held onto fear instead of trusting You. I know Your love is unshakable—it is not just a feeling, but a promise, an anchor, a foundation I can stand on.

Help me, Lord, to not be ruled by my emotions but to stand firm on Your truth, forgiveness, and freedom. Even when my heart resists, I choose to agree with Your Word rather than my fears. Transform my heart, Lord. Help me to forgive others—and even myself—just as You have forgiven me (Ephesians 4:31-32).

Jesus, give me the strength to release every hurt into Your hands. Protect my mind from the enemy's whispers—the ones that try to convince me that the pain is too deep, that the fear is too great, that the past still has power over me.

Lord, help me to put on the full armor of God, so I can stand firm against every lie and attack of the enemy (Ephesians 6). I know this battle is not mine to fight alone. Thank You for Your strength, Your protection, and the unshakable peace that comes from trusting You.

In Jesus' name,

Amen.

CHAPTER 4
Filling the Void

THE WEIGHT OF INVISIBLE CHAINS

It was a beautiful day—the kind of day that should have felt full of warmth and joy. Laughter filled the air, and the people around me seemed genuinely happy. I watched them, trying to absorb their lightheartedness, longing to feel the same way.

I turned my face toward the sun, hoping its heat would penetrate the coldness inside me—that maybe, just maybe, it would awaken something in me. But I felt nothing. No matter how hard I tried, I couldn't grasp the joy that seemed to come so naturally to everyone else.

I smiled. I even forced myself to try and participate, nodding, laughing at the right moments, trying to be present. But inside, I felt completely disconnected, like I was watching life happen through a window I couldn't break through. Why couldn't I just feel normal again?

A quiet frustration churned inside me—an ache of not knowing what to do, mixed with a sadness that felt like it was burrowing deeper into my soul. And the hardest part? I couldn't even explain why.

THE GROWING CLOUD

It wasn't like something terrible had happened. There wasn't a definite moment or singular traumatic event I could point to and say, "That's why I feel this way." Instead, it was like a small, lingering cloud that had been floating above me for a while—subtle at first, barely noticeable. But with each passing day, it gradually grew larger, darker, and heavier.

I kept telling myself it was nothing. Maybe I was just overly tired. Maybe I just needed a change. So I did what I had always done—I put on a cheerful face and carried on. I laughed. I joked. I talked about everyday things. But deep inside, I was becoming more isolated. I, at times, wondered if anyone noticed. Or, if I was being completely honest, if anyone even cared.

TORN BETWEEN TWO EMOTIONS

I longed for someone to look into my eyes and truly see me—not just the version I showed to the world, but the part silently struggling underneath. The part that carried a pressure I couldn't name, something that followed me no matter how hard I tried to shake it.

I hoped someone might see through the surface and understand the pain I couldn't explain. And there were times I tried—just a little. I'd mention that I was going through a rough patch or say I felt a bit down, maybe even bring up depression in passing. But I could never quite put it into words because I didn't fully understand it myself. And honestly, I didn't think they'd really understand either. Vulnerability felt too big, too exposing. So I'd quickly change the subject or brush it off with a laugh.

But deep down, I feared what might happen if someone truly saw the mess underneath my smiling exterior. I wasn't trying to lie or deceive anyone. I was just afraid. Afraid that if they knew the full truth, they might think less of me. That I would no longer seem strong or capable. That their view would change. I wasn't hiding out of dishonesty—I was hiding out of self-protection. But even that made me feel like a coward. And once that thought settled in, the self-defeating cycle would begin: guilt, shame, silence, repeat.

CHASING RELIEF

When you're desperate for relief, you'll reach for anything that seems like it might help. I know what it's like to search for something—to make the ache inside feel smaller. To try and fill the emptiness with distractions, achievements, or even relationships. For a little while, it worked. A new Jeep gave me a taste of freedom. A new job gave me a fresh focus—and for a time, I felt needed. For a moment, I believed I had found the thing that would finally fix what was broken inside me. But like reaching for the wrong kind of sweet when you're craving chocolate, none of it truly satisfies.

The emptiness always returned, stronger than before. And each time, it left me feeling even more lost and desperate. If the things I thought would help weren't enough, then what was? I kept searching, convinced that if I could just find the missing piece, I could put myself back together. But maybe the answer wasn't about finding more. Maybe it was about letting go. At the time, I wasn't ready to face that truth. Not yet.

A MOMENT OF HOPE

For a long time, I felt stuck in this cycle—believing it was my responsibility to fix myself, as if I had the power to heal what was unraveling inside me. But the harder I tried, the more I began to see the truth: healing was never mine to earn. It was always God's to give. Real freedom doesn't come from striving—it comes from surrender.

And friend, if you're in that place right now, I want you to hear this: this is not where your story ends. The enemy wants you to believe you'll always feel this way—that freedom isn't possible. But he is a liar.

The truth is, healing is possible. Freedom is possible. You don't have to have it all figured out today. You just have to take one small step toward hope. And you don't have to take it alone.

HEALING STEPS

If you've been carrying these feelings, I want you to know that you are not alone. If you've tried to "fix" yourself with distractions, success, or even relationships—you are not broken, and there is hope.

1. **Without shame, acknowledge what you're feeling.**

_____

_____

_____

_____

_____

_____

The first step to healing is being honest with yourself about what you're feeling.

I spent so much time denying, minimizing, or shaming myself for my emotions. But suppressing pain doesn't heal it—it only buries it deeper. God isn't waiting for you to "pull yourself together." He's waiting for you to bring your burdens to Him, just as you are.

2. **Ask Yourself:**

- Am I pretending I'm okay when I'm not? _____

- Have I been telling myself I "shouldn't" feel this way?_____

- What emotions am I pushing down instead of addressing?

_____

_____

_____

_____

_____

_____

_____

Bringing your burdens into the light takes away their power.

3. **Stop Reaching for Temporary Fixes**

Like the chocolate craving analogy didn't satisfy, temporary fixes will never bring lasting peace. I tried to fill my emptiness with distractions, accomplishments, and new experiences—but none of them were enough.

Maybe you've done the same thing. Maybe you've convinced yourself, *If I just had a better job, a relationship, a new start or rest more ... then I'd be happy.* But no matter how many times we try to fill a spiritual need with worldly solutions, it never works. Because only God can heal the deep places of your heart.

Ask Yourself:

Have I been looking for fulfillment in things that will never fully satisfy me?

_____

_____

_____

_____

_____

_____

_____

Am I using distractions to avoid dealing with my pain?

_____

_____

_____

_____

_____

_____

_____

What temporary "fixes" have I been running to instead of surrendering to God?

_____

_____

_____

_____

_____

_____

_____

Take a moment to pray. Tell God how you're feeling—even if it's messy, even if you don't have the right words. Healing doesn't happen overnight, but every step you take toward God is a step toward freedom.

SCRIPTURES

- "So letting your sinful nature control your mind leads to death. But letting the Spirit control your mind leads to life and peace." Romans 8:6

- "For the world offers only a craving for physical pleasure, a craving for everything we see, and pride in our achievements and possessions. These are not from the Father, but are from this world. And this world is fading away, along with everything that people crave. But anyone who does what pleases God will live forever." 1 John 2:16-17

- "The Lord is close to the brokenhearted; He rescues those whose spirits are crushed." Psalm 34:18

PRAYER PROMPT

A Prayer for Surrender and Healing

Heavenly Father,

Thank You for Your goodness and faithfulness. Even in my struggles, I know that You have never left me. Forgive me for the times I've tried to carry everything on my own, for the times I've turned to temporary solutions instead of turning to You. I realize now that I cannot fix myself, but I don't have to—because You are my Healer.

Lord, I ask for wisdom to recognize when I am under spiritual attack. Your Word tells us in Ephesians 6:10-18 to put on the armor of God, and I ask that You equip me to stand firm. Help me recognize the lies of the enemy so that I don't believe them as truth.

Give me the strength to release control and trust You with my healing. I don't want to keep running to things that will never satisfy—I want You, Lord.

Help me to focus on You and not the distractions of this world. Keep my heart pure before You. Let me not be consumed with the things of this world or try to fill my soul with things that can never replace You.

Thank You, Lord, for Your love, for Your guidance, and for the healing that You are bringing into my life, even now.

In Jesus' name,

Amen.

CHAPTER 5
Distorted Perspectives

I remembered noticing how distorted my own reflection had become—not in a mirror, but in how I viewed my life. Everything felt off, like I was walking through a fog, unable to trust what I was seeing.

All I could feel was: distorted perspectives.

THE FUNHOUSE MIRROR: WHEN FEAR AND DEPRESSION DISTORT REALITY

Not long ago, Vernon and I wandered into a fun little shop—the kind filled with vintage trinkets, antiques, and odd little treasures that made you pause and take a second look. As we wandered through the aisles, something caught our attention—a carnival-style funhouse mirror. We stood in front of it, laughing at the strange, warped reflections staring back at us. One moment, my legs stretched impossibly long, my torso barely there. The next, my head looked gigantic while the rest of me seemed to disappear. Every small movement changed the way I looked, making me appear ridiculous and completely distorted.

At the time, it was just funny. I tucked the moment away as something silly, but later that night, I couldn't shake the image. That warped reflection stayed with me—not because it made me laugh, but because it felt strangely familiar.

That mirror reminded me of how I felt during my hardest season. Depression doesn't just affect how we feel—it distorts how we see ourselves. It twists our perspective until even the smallest things look bigger, heavier, and more hopeless than they really are.

- The weight of tasks that once felt simple, now overwhelming.

- The distance in conversations where I was physically present but emotionally gone.

- The ache of a sadness I couldn't explain—and couldn't shake.

- The emptiness in moments that should have brought joy, but didn't.

- The silence of private battles, even as life moved forward around me.

And just like the mirror, the longer I focused on that distorted image, the easier it was to believe it. I had become so consumed with what I felt. I forgot what was true.

When Fear and Depression Distort Reality

Just like that funhouse mirror twisted and bent my reflection, fear and depression distorts the way we see ourselves, others, and the world around us.

- They magnify our mistakes, making them feel larger than life—overshadowing everything else.

- They blur out the good, making it hard to remember our blessings.

- They whisper lies, convincing us that things will never change, that we are alone, that we are unworthy.

And over time, those distortions start to feel like the truth. I remember a particular season in my life when I felt trapped in an endless replay of past failures. Just like looking into a carnival mirror, the reflection I saw was far from accurate. This isn't just something I've experienced—it's something many of us face.

- Fear came right alongside depression, amplifying the distortion.

- Fear whispered, "What if this is who you really are?"

- Fear told me, "You'll never be enough."

- Fear reminded me, "Things will never change."

I kept replaying past moments, questioning my worth, wondering if anything I had done truly mattered. I was exhausted, discouraged, and I didn't know how to break free. But here's what I learned: the reflection I saw was not the full picture. Even when my emotions told me otherwise, God's truth about me had not changed. I had spent so much time staring at a distorted reflection, I forgot there was another way to see. God wasn't looking at me through the lens of failure—He saw me through grace, through truth, through love.

Reaching for Support: The Power of Community

Even though I knew deep down that my perspective was off, I couldn't seem to break free from it. The more I fought against the lies in my mind, the stronger they seemed to grow. I prayed. I tried to push through. But the loneliness only made the weight heavier. That's when I realized something had to change—I couldn't fight this battle alone.

I had spent too long staring into the mirror of distortion, letting it define me, shape my thoughts, and cloud my vision. The weight of it all felt unbearable, and no matter how hard I tried to silence the lies in my head, they only seemed to grow louder. I told myself I should be able to handle it on my own. But the truth is I couldn't.

Remember, the enemy wants to isolate us.

At first, I leaned on my husband—his love and support were unwavering. But deep down, I knew the weight I was carrying was too heavy for one person to bear with me. I needed a wider circle of support.

So, I did something I had been avoiding for far too long: I reached out further. I opened up to my sister, my sister-in-law, and just a few friends. And let me tell you—it wasn't easy. Admitting my struggle felt like exposing a wound I had worked hard to keep hidden. I was afraid of what they would think. Would they see me as weak? Would they look at me differently?

But when I finally let my guard down ... they didn't turn away. They didn't offer clichés or quick fixes. They simply saw me. They met me in my pain, without judgment, without pretense, without conditions. Instead, they wrapped me in love and truth. They reminded me of who I truly was—the person I had lost sight of. They saw the good in me when I couldn't. They spoke words of hope when I felt I had none left.

And even though the depression didn't magically disappear, something began to shift. I wasn't fighting alone anymore. For the first time in a long time, I saw a glimmer of hope break through my darkness.

THROUGH GOD'S EYES: WHEN THE LIES FEEL LOUDER THAN TRUTH

The room is quiet as you scroll through your phone. Without even realizing it, you're comparing your life to perfectly curated pictures and highlight reels of social media. We don't always go looking for comparison, but it still finds its way in—whether it's through a screen, a conversation, or a quiet moment of self-doubt. It looks different for everyone, but the effect is often the same: we start questioning our worth.

The thoughts creep in so easily: "*You'll never be enough.*" "*You're falling behind.*" You may not be searching for validation, but deep down, you're hoping something will make you feel better. Something to quiet the ache, to make you feel a little less behind and a little more okay.

The enemy is subtle. He doesn't have to shout—he just whispers the same lies over and over until they start to sound like truth. And the less time we spend in God's presence, the easier it is to believe them.

Sometimes that distance from God comes from distraction. But other times, it comes from something more consuming, something deeper. Sometimes, it's depression. Depression has a way of making God feel far away. It clouds your mind, drains your energy, and makes even simple prayers feel impossible. You might know, deep down, that He's still there, but it's hard to feel Him when everything feels numb.

If you've ever felt this way, you're not alone. David did too. In Psalm 42, he pours out his sorrow and confusion, crying:

"'O God my rock,' I cry, 'why have you forgotten me? Why must I wander around in grief, oppressed by my enemies?'" (Psalm 42:9)

Even though David knew God was faithful, his pain made him feel abandoned. But here's what's powerful: he didn't stop there. In the very same Psalm, he speaks truth back to his soul:

"Why am I discouraged? Why is my heart so sad? I will put my hope in God! I will praise him again—my Savior and my God!" (Psalm 42:11)

David teaches us something vital: even when you can't feel God, you can still reach for Him. Even when your emotions scream that He's distant, His presence hasn't left. Even when the darkness feels overwhelming, His light is still there.

The enemy wants you to believe that depression separates you from God—but nothing can separate you from His love.

"I am convinced that nothing can ever separate us from God's love ... neither our fears for today nor our worries about tomorrow ..." Romans 8:38

So if you feel distant, if prayer feels hard, if worship feels empty, don't turn away. Press in. Even if all you can say is, *"God, I need You."* That's enough. Because the closer you stay to Him—even in the silence—the more His truth will break through the lies.

SPEAKING TRUTH, EVEN WHEN YOU DON'T FEEL IT

When the enemy's lies have been playing on repeat in your mind, it's not always easy to believe the truth. Maybe you've been told you're not enough. That your past defines you. That you've drifted too far for God to bring you back. Over time, those words can sink in and start to shape how you see yourself.

But the truth is this: what God says about you is unshakable—no matter how you feel.

Your name isn't written in pencil, easily erased. It's not scribbled in disappearing ink. It's engraved—permanently etched into the hands of the One who made you.

"See, I have written your name on the palms of my hands." (Isaiah 49:16)

Still, there's a difference between knowing that in your head and believing it in your heart. That's why Scripture tells us to renew our minds:

"Let God transform you into a new person by changing the way you think." (Romans 12:2)

Transformation doesn't happen when we finally feel worthy—it begins when we start to align our thoughts with God's truth. So how do you begin that process?

You start by learning to speak God's Word over yourself. Even when it feels unnatural. Even when it feels hollow. Even when you don't fully believe it yet. Because truth remains truth, even when you don't feel it. God's presence and faithfulness aren't tied to your emotions.

Write down Scriptures about your identity in Christ. Put them where you'll see them—on sticky notes, in your journal, on your phone. And when doubt creeps in, speak them out loud:

- "O Lord, you have examined my heart and know everything about me. You know when I sit down or stand up. You know my thoughts even when I'm far away." (Psalm 139:1–2)

- "I have loved you with an everlasting love." Jeremiah 31:3 (NIV)

- "My grace is all you need. My power works best in weakness." 2 Corinthians 12:9

At first, it may feel like you're just repeating words. But over time, the more you replace lies with truth, the more you begin to see yourself the way God sees you.

The deeper His Word takes root in your heart, the clearer your vision becomes—not through the lens of depression, comparison, or shame, but through the eyes of the One who created you, knows you, and calls you His own.

RETRAINING MINDSET: SHIFTING OUR FOCUS

One of the most powerful ways I've learned to shift my focus is by keeping a journal specifically, by making two lists each day.

- One for your burdens – the things that weigh on your heart and mind.
- One for your blessings – the reminders of God's faithfulness.

At first, the burden list may seem overwhelming. The gratitude list? Almost an afterthought. But as you continue this practice, something remarkable begins to happen. Even in the hardest seasons, you will start to see God's hand at work. Even in the silence, His presence will become undeniable.

Some days, your gratitude list may seem simple:

- A hot cup of coffee.
- A sunrise stretching across the sky.
- An unexpected text or call from a friend at just the right moment.

But these "small" things are not small at all. They are whispers of His love. They are evidence of His nearness.

A dear friend recently shared something that really stuck with me. She said that when she walks into a room and forgets why she's there, instead of getting frustrated or criticizing herself up, she takes it as a cue to thank God—whether for eventually reminding her what she came in for, or simply for already meeting her needs that day in other ways.

What a beautiful shift in perspective, a reminder that even when life feels hard to bear, you are not alone. Rather than letting forgetfulness become a source of self-criticism, she turns it into an act of worship. Instead of seeing it as a moment of weakness, she sees it as a moment of Godly provision. This is the heart of retraining our mindset: learning to see every moment, even the frustrating ones, through the lens of God's presence.

What if we did the same? What if, in the middle of our stress, exhaustion, and forgetfulness, we turned first to gratitude? What if we stopped seeing our shortcomings as failures and started seeing them as opportunities to lean into His grace? What if, instead of criticizing ourselves—*"I'm so stupid," "I can't do anything right," "Why am I like this?"*—we began to speak blessings instead? What if we reminded ourselves, *"I am still learning," "God is with me in this," "His strength is made perfect in my weakness?"*

This isn't about ignoring reality—it's about reclaiming it. Speaking truth in the face of distortion. It's one of the ways we begin to see ourselves as God sees us, even when the reflection we see is warped. Scripture tells us, "Be thankful in all circumstances, for this is God's will for you who belong to Christ Jesus." (1 Thessalonians 5:18)

Gratitude doesn't ignore the pain—it redirects our focus. It lifts our eyes off ourselves and onto the God who is faithful and present, even in the hardest places.

If you have been struggling to see beyond the weight of life, start here. Write them down—both the burdens and the blessings, the small and the big things. Because in writing, in remembering, in the naming of what is true, you will begin to shift your focus from the weight of what you carry to the faithfulness of the One who carries it with you.

The more you practice gratitude, the more you begin to see what God has been saying all along. If you've been believing the lie that God is distant, unloving, or uninterested in your life—it's time to replace it with truth.

- **God has not abandoned you**.
  Hebrews 13:5 says, "I will never fail you. I will never abandon you."

- **God will not forget you.**
  Isaiah 44:21 says, "Pay attention, O Jacob, for you are my servant, O Israel. I, the Lord, made you, and I will not forget you"

- **God has not stopped loving you.**
  Psalm 89:33 says, "But I will never stop loving him nor fail to keep my promise to him."

- **You are fully known.**
  Psalm 139:1 says, "O Lord, you have examined my heart and know everything about me."

- **You are deeply loved.**
  Psalm 63:3 says, "Your unfailing love is better than life itself, how I praise you!"

- **You are His.**
  Psalm 100:3 says, "Know that the Lord is God. It is he who made us, and we are his; we are his people."

Even if you don't feel it yet, speak His truth over yourself anyway. His Word is the only mirror that will ever show you who you truly are.

PRAYER PROMPT

Dear Heavenly Father,

Shatter the mirror of lies I've been believing. Destroy every root that has tried to wrap around me and hold me captive. Replace what I feel with what You've said. Let Your truth rise above the noise in my mind.

When fear whispers that I'm not enough, remind me that I am Yours. When depression tries to distort my view, lift my eyes to focus on You. Let Your Word become the only mirror I trust.

Erase what the enemy tried to use for harm, and repaint my future with the vibrant colors of Your promises filled with truth, hope, and freedom. Remove the smears of shame, regret, and fear, every stain the enemy tried to use to define me.

My God, You are greater. You are stronger than all!

Stronger than the lies.

Stronger than the past.

Stronger than anything that tries to keep me bound.

My heart overflows with thankfulness and gratitude for Your presence during this difficult time.

Thank You, Lord! In Jesus' name,

Amen.

CHAPTER 6

Releasing a False Sense of Control

Have you ever felt like something was missing—like everyone else had some key piece of the puzzle that you just couldn't find? Looking back, I realize that was me. I knew who God was. I believed in His power. Yet somehow, I wasn't fully living in that truth.

My view of Him—and of myself—had become clouded. Fear, worry, and distraction blurred everything. One by one, they pulled me deeper into a place of exhaustion and despair, and I found myself slipping into depression. The pressure of it all began to consume me, and I couldn't see Jesus as clearly as I once had—or as desperately as I needed to.

For a long time, I thought I could fix it by changing things around me. If I could just reset my routine, rearrange my life, or find the right "solution," then maybe I could ease the tension I felt inside. I kept thinking that if I could control the chaos on the outside, I could calm the fear within.

But no matter what I changed, the same fear and sadness followed me. They wrapped around my heart like chains, keeping me bound in a cycle of striving, overthinking, and chasing after peace that never lasted. I had started to believe the lie that it was all up to me to hold everything together.

THE JEEP RIDE: A SEASON OF DARKNESS

We had taken the Jeep out for a ride—something we've always enjoyed. The open air, the sense of freedom, the rush of simply being alive had always been an appreciated gift. It was usually one of those small things that helped clear my mind, let me breathe a little deeper. The beauty of creation often felt like a much-needed embrace from God.

But that day, something was different. The familiar roads didn't bring the same peace. The warm breeze that once made me feel light and free felt distant, like I was watching someone else's life from a window I couldn't open.

I could hear Vernon talking beside me—his voice steady, familiar. In the distance, the hum of a lawnmower mingled with the barking of a neighbor's dog. Up ahead, the trees danced to a tune we couldn't hear—unbothered, untouched, as if my world wasn't caving in around me.

I had been putting on a brave face, staying busy, pretending to be okay. But inside, something had been unraveling. The gradual gray I had been pushing through had darkened into something deeper—something that slowly began to consume me. A wave of sadness settled deep in my chest, suffocating me. And beneath it, something even heavier. Depression. Fear. Hopelessness.

As we pulled into our garage, something inside me broke. The weight I had been carrying—all the silence, the sadness, the pretending—crashed down at once. I couldn't hold it in anymore. Tears spilled over, raw and unstoppable, as I gasped for breath between uneven sobs. The pain was so heavy, I could barely speak, but I managed to whisper the words that had been building inside me: *"I just can't seem to find my way back to who I was."*

It was true. My chest ached with the sadness of it. I missed the version of me who wasn't always exhausted. The one who didn't wake up already feeling defeated. The one who laughed easily and felt deeply without fear.

She was familiar. Comfortable. Whole—or at least, I thought she was.

I had tried. I had fought. But still, I felt like I had lost her. And for the first time, I was terrified that maybe … I never would get her back.

Then in the wreckage of my desperation, a whisper cut through the noise in my mind: *"You were never meant to go back."* It was like a rock being dropped into the depths of my soul—each ripple bringing a quiet realization that began to stir something new in me.

Looking back now, I can see it clearly—it was a nugget of truth straight from God, one that opened my eyes. Because the version of me I was longing for—the one I thought I had lost—had never truly been free. I was still bound. Still carrying suppressed fear, depression, and the lies the enemy had planted deep in my heart. I had known joy. I had loved deeply. Life had held beauty before— but buried beneath it all was pain I hadn't yet faced. And over time, it quietly built into a storm I didn't see coming. I hadn't been fully living—I was moving through life on autopilot, just trying to hold it all together.

All that time, I had been facing the wrong direction— grieving who I used to be, desperately straining to reclaim a version of myself that God never asked me to return to. And in doing so, I nearly missed the person He was trying to lead me to become.

He wasn't calling me back. He was inviting me forward—to let go of the false comfort of the familiar and step into something greater. Something healed. Something whole.

The version of me I had been mourning was still trying to hold everything together. Still convinced I had to figure it all out. Still gripping my Burdens, trying to carry what God never meant for me to hold. God was rebuilding someone new—someone rooted in truth, no longer driven by fear and sorrow.

I couldn't see it then, but He was moving. Quietly. Faithfully. Shifting my focus from what I couldn't fix to the One who never changes.

And friend, maybe that's true for you, too. Maybe you've been searching—trying to get back to the person you were before the heartache, before the anxiety, before the weight of life settled in.

Have you found yourself reaching for who you used to be—before the fear, before the burnout, before everything changed? But what if God isn't calling you back ... what if He's inviting you forward?

What if, even now, He's doing something new?

"See, I am doing a new thing! Now it springs up; do you not perceive it?" (Isaiah 43:19, NIV)

LOSING SIGHT OF MY ANCHOR

Pastor Ben Bausback, an assistant pastor at my church, the Bridge of Hope, once shared a story that resonated deeply within me. As a child, he had been floating along in a lazy river, safe and secure, wrapped in the comfort of the water—everything suddenly changed. He slipped off his float and plunged beneath the surface.

For a moment, he was completely submerged, disoriented and gasping, unsure of which way was up. When he finally broke through the surface for air, panic set in. His mother—his source of safety, his anchor—was nowhere in sight. The steady presence he had relied on felt gone. He thrashed in the water, searching desperately, with his heart pounding. In that moment, nothing else mattered but knowing he wasn't alone. And then, just when fear threatened to take over, he saw her. She had never left. She was right there, waiting for him.

That story mirrored something I hadn't fully recognized until then in my own journey. Life hit me hard—one wave after another. There were unexpected losses, strained relationships, and the slow, creeping fear that I was failing the people I loved. The pressure built until I couldn't breathe under it.

And when I finally came up for air, I realized something painful: I had lost sight of my anchor. I couldn't see Jesus, not because He had moved but because I had stopped looking in His direction. I reached for anything that felt solid, anything that could make me feel like I wasn't completely unraveling. I chased control, believing that if I could just organize my world perfectly, I'd feel safe again. I clung tightly to perfectionism, hoping that flawless performance could silence the chaos inside me. I buried myself in distractions, tasks, people, noise, anything to drown out the rising fear. I was desperate to find something that could steady me, something that wouldn't shift beneath my feet. But no matter what I grabbed onto, nothing held. Everything slipped through my fingers, and I was left more anxious, more exhausted, more afraid than before.

I was like Peter when he stepped out of the boat to walk on water toward Jesus (Matthew 14:29-31). As long as his eyes were fixed on Christ, he walked on water in faith. But the moment he focused on the storm, fear pulled him under. That was me. The more I tried to manage the storm myself, the more I sank.

THE TRAP OF PERFECTIONISM

Perfectionism is a sneaky kind of bondage. It dresses itself up as discipline and high standards, but underneath, it's driven by fear. It told me that if I just tried harder, performed better, and held everything together, I could finally find peace. But that was a lie. The deeper I sank into it, the more it fed my fears—fear of failure, fear of letting others down, fear that I was never enough.

Only God is perfect. The peace I so desperately longed for wasn't found in how well I performed; it was found in how deeply I trusted. God was so patient with me—so kind in the way He began to peel back the layers. He wasn't demanding perfection. He was inviting me to rest in Him.

CARRYING WHAT WASN'T MINE

For a long time, I tried to hold things that were never mine to carry. I poured myself into fixing what I couldn't control. I thought if I just worked harder, planned better, stayed one step ahead, I could change outcomes—prevent pain—protect everyone I loved. But Jesus asks a simple, piercing question:

"Can any one of you by worrying add a single hour to your life?" (Matthew 6:27, NIV)

I knew the answer, yet I lived as if worry was my responsibility and outcomes were my burden to bear. The weight of it all slowly wore me down—not because I was weak, but because I was carrying what wasn't meant for me.

Through grace, God began to show me the truth: I can't fix people. I can't foresee or prevent every loss. I can't be the hero of every story. But I can pray. I can trust. I can release what was never mine to begin with. And when I did? I could finally breathe again. Not perfectly. Not all at once. But deeply for the first time in a long time.

Can I gently ask, is there something in your life right now that you're holding too tightly? Something you've been gripping with everything you've got, hoping that if you just hold on long enough, you can hold it all together?

THE POWER OF THE BURDEN BALLOON

I mentioned previously that during that season, God gave me a simple but powerful image that's now part of my daily walk with Him. It's a Burden Balloon. Throughout the day, I imagine placing my worries, fears, and unspoken concerns inside it—each one acknowledged, each one held in the presence of God. It becomes a kind of spiritual container, holding what I can't fix or figure out.

But as I mentioned before, if I don't release it—if I keep filling it without surrendering—the weight of it all begins to pull me down. The balloon that was meant to lift begins to sink. And so do I. That's when I know it's time. Time to let go—again.

In prayer, I open my hands. I picture the balloon rising—higher and higher—until it's beyond my reach, carried by the One who never grows tired, never forgets, and never asks me to hold what He's already willing to carry. It's not about pretending the burdens don't exist. It's about acknowledging them and then trusting God with them.

"Come to me, all you who are weary and burdened, and I will give you rest." (Matthew 11:28, NIV)

Not a new plan, not more effort, just rest.

That kind of rest doesn't come from control. It comes from trust. And every time I release that balloon, I'm reminded of God's willingness to take it.

SURRENDERING THE ILLUSION OF CONTROL

Surrender wasn't a single turning point for me—it became a daily routine. Some mornings, the old patterns try to creep back in: *You should know what to do. You're the one holding this together. Don't drop the ball.* But now, I meet those lies with truth.

My identity isn't rooted in how much I accomplish. My peace isn't tied to predictable outcomes.

My safety doesn't come from having control—it comes from trusting a faithful God. God promises, "You will keep in perfect peace those whose minds are steadfast, because they trust in you." (Isaiah 26:3, NIV)

And He is keeping me—not because I figured it all out, but because I chose to let go. I still picture that balloon—floating above the chaos I once tried to manage. Not as a magic fix, but as a sacred exchange. One more reminder that peace isn't found in perfection; it's found in His presence.

Pastor Ben's story continues to echo in my heart: when we lose sight of our anchor, fear sets in. But Jesus never leaves. Even when we drift, He remains steady, ready to draw us back into His peace. So now, when fear rises or darkness presses in, I pause. I breathe. I picture that balloon again—rising, weightless, free—and I remember:

I don't have to carry it anymore.

Surrender doesn't mean I've stopped caring—it means I've finally trusted God enough to stop trying to be Him. If you're reading this and you feel worn out from trying to hold it all together, hear this:

You're not supposed to.

Letting go isn't the end of the story—it's the beginning of healing. Surrender didn't erase all my pain, but it opened the door to a process that was deeper, truer, and more freeing than anything I'd ever known. It didn't make life easy, but it made me whole.

God wasn't just undoing old patterns. He was forming something new in me. And what came next wouldn't just challenge me, and thankfully, it would change me.

HEALING STEPS

1. **What situation am I gripping tightly instead of trusting God with?** Write down the worry or burden you struggle to release. This is for your Burden Balloon.

_____

_____

_____

_____

_____

_____

Hold it in your hands—imagine its weight. In prayer, visualize loosening your grip and letting it rise, trusting God to carry what you cannot. As a tangible reminder, place your written note of your struggle, in a jar, your Bible, or another visible spot—symbolizing that it no longer belongs to you but to Him.

SCRIPTURES

Trusting God is central to overcoming your fear and depression. His Word tells us in

- "But when I am afraid, I will put my trust in you. I praise God for what he has promised. I trust in God, so why should I be afraid?" Psalm 56:3-4

- "He heals the brokenhearted and bandages their wounds." Psalm 147:3

- "The gatekeeper opens the gate for him, and the sheep recognize his voice and come to him. He calls His own sheep by name and leads them out." John 10:3

PRAYER PROMPT

Lord,

I come to You with a heart full of gratitude—for Your love, grace, and the way You see me, even when I struggle to see myself clearly. Thank You for loving me not just in my best moments, but in my broken ones as well. Even when I feel unlovable, You call me chosen, worthy, and Yours.

But Lord, I confess—my thoughts are not always kind. Sometimes, they are heavy, unfiltered, and filled with things I wish weren't there. They can be harsh toward myself, unfair toward others, and darkened by the weight of my surroundings.

Forgive me, Lord, for the times I have believed the lie that I could handle things on my own. For the times I have relied on my own strength instead of Yours, when I have clung to control instead of surrendering to You. Forgive me for carrying burdens that were never mine to bear.

Lord, help me to know the difference between being there for someone in need and trying to "fix" what is not mine to fix. Teach me to love and support others without stepping into a role that belongs only to You. Give me the wisdom to know when to speak, when to listen, and when to simply pray.

Give me the strength to trust You completely and to let go of the things in my Burden Balloon. Help me to release the weight of worry, fear, and control, and to entrust them fully into Your care. I know that I am not meant to carry these things, and I surrender them to You now.

Please clear my vision, Lord. Let me see myself, others, and my circumstances through Your truth, not through the fog of fear, depression, or the enemy's lies. Break the stranglehold that has gripped my mind and spirit—help me breathe again. Let Your peace fill the spaces where fear and depression have settled.

Give me clarity where there is confusion. Give me peace where there is unrest. Give me strength where I feel weak.

And Father, help me take the steps I need to heal. I know that renewing my mind and breaking unhealthy patterns takes effort, but I can't do it without You. Give me the energy, the determination, and the discipline to put in the work—physically, mentally, and spiritually. Help me choose truth over lies, hope over despair, and faith over fear.

I surrender this battle to You, Lord.

In Jesus' name,

Amen.

CHAPTER 7
Light Up the Darkness

"The light shines in the darkness, and the darkness can never extinguish it."

John 1:5

A PRAYER & SURRENDER

I felt the pull and I understood it. It wasn't just emotion. It wasn't just the weight of my struggles catching up with me. It was something stronger, God was drawing me.

I sat there, my heart pounding, my hands clenched in my lap. A war raged inside me. Part of me wanted to stay put, to hold everything in, to pretend I was fine. But another part of me, the part that was weary from carrying it all alone, knew I couldn't stay where I was.

And then, before I could stop myself, I stood up. Tears blurred my vision as I stepped into the aisle. My legs felt unsteady beneath me, but something greater than my fear and depression was leading me forward. Every step toward the altar felt like a release, a surrender I had been too afraid to give before. By the time I reached the front, the tears were already starting to fall.

Sue Thurston, a visiting World Missionary, turned to me, her eyes full of compassion, and gently placed her hands on my shoulders. Her voice was steady, filled with faith, as she began to pray over me. Her words weren't just words; they were cutting through the chains I had been carrying for far too long. She prayed for Jesus to break the bondage of fear. To release me from its grip and to restore what had been stolen.

But as Sue prayed, and as God's presence pressed in, I felt the first fracture. The walls I had built to hold myself together weren't protecting me; they were imprisoning me. And in that moment, surrender didn't feel like weakness—it felt like the light of Jesus shattering my darkness.

I knelt at the altar as the tears poured freely, but they weren't just of sorrow: they were sweet tears of release. My body trembled under the weight of His presence; His nearness was unmistakable. I knew God was doing something deep. I couldn't name every chain at that moment, but I could feel them loosening. Strongholds I had lived with for years were beginning to break.

And while my encounter happened at the front of a church that day, please don't think you have to be in a building like that for God to meet you. His power isn't limited to an altar. He'll meet you in your car, your kitchen, your quiet moments, or your most chaotic ones. The place doesn't matter—His presence does.

I didn't have all the answers. I didn't know what tomorrow would bring. But I knew one thing: I wasn't alone. I had no more strength, no more words, and no more pretending. I couldn't fix it. I couldn't figure it out—and finally, I didn't have to.

And for the first time, I truly saw that I was at a crossroads. I could keep clinging to control, pretending I had it all together ... or I could surrender, fully and completely. I had finally reached the end of myself and that's exactly where God met me.

This wasn't about saying the perfect prayer. It wasn't about dramatic emotion or doing the right thing in front of others. It was real. Raw. Holy. I whispered the only thing I could:

"Help me, Jesus. Help me, Jesus. I can't do this anymore."

That was all I had. But somehow, I knew—it was enough.

THE BLOOD THAT HEALS

In the quiet after my prayer, truth rose in my spirit—firm and clear, like a light cutting through fog:

"But he was pierced for our rebellion, crushed for our sins. He was beaten so we could be whole. He was whipped so we could be healed." (Isaiah 53:5)

That verse wasn't new to me. I had read it, quoted it, even prayed it before. But in that moment, it wasn't just a verse—it was my lifeline. His blood was enough. Enough to cover the past I couldn't undo. Enough to touch the wounds I had learned to hide. Enough to lift the weight I no longer had strength to carry.

Jesus wasn't asking me to fix myself. He wasn't waiting for me to prove anything. He was simply asking me to trust what He had already done ... was more than enough. I didn't need to earn my healing. I just needed to surrender to it.

And friend, that healing is for you too. No matter how broken you feel. No matter how many times you've failed. No matter how long you've been stuck in the same cycle. The blood of Jesus hasn't lost its power. It still heals. It still restores. It still sets people free.

The only question is: Will you let go?

Will you stop trying to carry it on your own? Will you surrender—not just your sin, but your sorrow, your anxiety, your fear, your striving? Because even now, I believe Jesus is drawing you. Just like He drew me.

He sees the pain behind your strength. He knows the weight you hide from everyone else.

And He's not waiting for you to figure it out—He's simply inviting you to trust that He is enough.

FEAR EXPOSED

And suddenly, it struck me—this wasn't the first time I had cried out those words.

I had whispered to them before, on a different day, in a different kind of battle. I remembered being overwhelmed at work, feeling the pressure close in like a wave. I had wanted to run. I couldn't think clearly. I couldn't breathe. And in that moment, just like at the altar, I had whispered, *"Help me, Jesus. Help me, Jesus."*

He had been faithful then. And He was faithful now.

Looking back, I could see how He had been walking with me the whole time. I hadn't ended up at that altar by accident—I had been led there. Prayer by prayer. Breakdown by breakdown. Moment by moment. He had never stopped pursuing me.

Though I had given my life to Christ as a child, this moment was something different. It wasn't about salvation for eternity—it was about rescue in the here and now. I needed Jesus to step in and deliver me. To break the chains I hadn't even known were still holding me.

I had gone forward to receive prayer. But as the evangelist began to pray—someone who didn't know my story—she began to speak directly to fear. She prayed against it with clarity and boldness, as if

God had placed the word on her heart just for me.

But I didn't recognize it at the time. In that moment, I was consumed with survival. I was just trying to breathe through the weight of it all. Her words stirred something in me, but I couldn't name it yet. It wasn't until a day or two later, in the quiet, that I finally saw it clearly: *Fear had been there all along.*

It had been hiding behind my exhaustion. Feeding my anxiety. Fueling the depression I thought was the whole story. But fear was the root I hadn't seen—because I had been so focused on surviving.

It wasn't just emotion. It had become a stronghold—a fear so deeply rooted that it had shaped the way I lived, even without me realizing it.

Fear had shaped the way I thought, the way I reacted, the way I coped. It had blended into my identity so well, I didn't even recognize it as separate from me. But God did. And in His mercy, He started to bring it into the light—not to shame me, but to heal me.

Can I gently ask—have you taken a moment to look beneath your own burdens? Could there be something deeper driving the weight you carry? What if the racing thoughts, the endless striving, or the emotional heaviness is rooted in fear—fear that says you're not allowed to let go? That if you stop holding everything together, it will all fall apart?

Jesus is ready to break those chains.

JESUS, THE LIGHT IN MY DARKNESS

As I reached up in desperation in prayer, God reached down in power. Jesus began to cut through the fog I had been living in, through the fear, the anxiety, and the depression that had wrapped themselves so tightly around me. His presence didn't just comfort me; it confronted what had been holding me captive. He started to unravel the lies I had believed for far too long.

It was like He was clearing out a dense forest of fear—tearing down strong trees of insecurity and uprooting the roots of pain that had grown deep beneath the surface. I had spent so much time trying to trim back symptoms, but He was going after the **source**. He wasn't just helping me feel better. He was making me new.

And friend, He can do the same for you.

Jesus is not intimidated by your darkness. He doesn't flinch at your fear. He comes with light that pierces through every shadow. His presence is strong enough to reach the places you've buried, the ones you've tried to forget, and the ones you didn't even know were broken.

He's not waiting for you to get it all together. Jesus is simply waiting for your surrender. And friend, He can do the same for you. Jesus is reaching out His hand—will you take it?

Finally Letting Go

One by one, God began to lift the burdens I had carried for far too long:

- My deep fear of losing a child.
- My fear of failure.
- My constant need to fix what I could never control.

That morning, I walked away from the altar differently, lighter. I didn't drag my Burden Balloon back to my seat. For the first time in a long time, I truly knew: I wasn't carrying those burdens anymore. I had finally released them to the only One strong enough to hold them.

The streaks of mascara on my face were no longer signs of despair—they were evidence of freedom. Of joy. Of healing. I smiled, and this time, it wasn't forced. It wasn't covering anything up. It was real. God had graciously given me peace … and a genuine smile I hadn't felt in a long time.

As sweet as that moment was, in the days that followed, I began to realize something important: Surrender wasn't the finish line—it was the starting point. Yes, I had released my burdens to God. But now God was inviting me deeper, into trust and transformation. The healing had begun, but the refining was just beginning.

Because true freedom isn't just about letting go of what weighs you down—it's about letting God reshape what's inside you. And that process? It's beautiful. It's holy. And sometimes, it's really hard.

But it's worth it.

HEALING STEPS

1. **Have I fully surrendered these burdens to Jesus, or am I still holding onto some of them?**

---

2. Be honest. If surrender feels difficult, ask God to help you let go.
   How has fear influenced my life without me realizing it?

_____

_____

_____

_____

_____

_____

_____

3. What does true freedom in Christ mean for me?

_____

_____

_____

_____

_____

_____

4. What truth from God's Word can I hold onto when the enemy tries to pull me back into fear?

_____

_____

_____

_____

_____

_____

_____

SCRIPTURE

"But everyone who calls on the name of the Lord will be saved." Joel 2:32

This Scripture took on a new and deeper meaning for me. It's not only about the salvation of our soul for eternal life—as miraculous as that is—but also about the saving grace and strength God gives us daily.

When we call on Him in our desperation, in our brokenness, in our darkest moments—He hears us. He saves us. Not just once, but again and again. Every time we whisper, *"Help me, Jesus."* Every time we fall to our knees and surrender. He meets us right there.

"The faithful love of the Lord never ends! His mercies never cease. Great is his faithfulness; his mercies begin afresh each morning." (Lamentations 3:22-23)

No matter how heavy our load has been, God's love remains constant. Even when we've drifted, when we feel like we're too broken, too exhausted, too far gone—His mercies are new every morning. That means right now. That means this very moment. If you feel like you're at your breaking point, His mercy is waiting for you.

PRAYER PROMPT

Dear Lord,

Thank You for hearing me when I call. Thank You for meeting me in my brokenness and lifting my burdens. I no longer have to live in fear. You have set me free. I no longer have to try to fix things in my own strength. You are my strength. I no longer have to carry what was never mine to bear. You are my burden-bearer.

Lord, I praise You because Your blood has washed over me, Your mercy has renewed me, and Your love has restored me. When the enemy tries to whisper old lies, remind me of the truth—I am no longer bound. I am free. I choose to walk forward in the peace and joy You have given me.

I plead the precious blood of Jesus over my mind, my body, and my spirit—not in desperation, but in victory. I will praise You because You have done what I could never do on my own.

In Jesus' name,

Amen.

CHAPTER 8
Refining Fire

THE PURPOSE OF THE FIRE

I had thought surrender would be the hardest part. That once I finally let go, everything would fall into place. But I was beginning to learn—surrender is just the starting point. It's what leads us into the fire … not to destroy us but to refine us.

Fire is powerful. It has the ability to consume, but it also has the ability to transform. It can destroy, but it can also purify, strengthen, and renew. And that's exactly what God's refining fire does in our lives: "I will refine them like silver and test them like gold." (Zechariah 13:9, NIV)

In ancient times, a silversmith would heat raw silver over a fire, melting away impurities, watching closely as the dross or impurities were burned off. The process continued until the refiner could see his own reflection in the silver.

That's how God works in us. The refining fire of trials isn't meant to destroy us—but to remove what doesn't belong so that we can reflect Jesus more clearly.

But let's be honest—refining is painful. We don't get to choose when the fire comes, and we certainly don't get to control how long it lasts. And the challenge is, it's hard to see what God is doing.

WALKING THROUGH THE FIRE

If you've ever faced a trial that left you questioning everything, you know what it's like to walk through the fire.

At first, I thought I could just push through and be okay. I didn't realize I was in the middle of a refining process. But refining isn't about rushing through—it's about surrendering to the process. And some days, the process felt unbearable. There were nights I lay awake, feeling the weight of fear and depression pressing in. The lies of the enemy whispered relentlessly: *"You'll never be free from this. You'll always be this broken. What if this is the night something happens?"*

Have you ever heard those same lies? The fire can feel like a furnace of isolation—quiet, consuming, and deafening—where the enemy tries to convince us that we are alone. But that's the biggest lie of all. Because we are never alone in the fire. Jesus is in it with us. I couldn't see the path, but He never lost sight of me. I felt like I was breaking, but He never let me go.

And right now—He's holding you, too.

"When you walk through the fire, you will not be burned; the flames will not set you ablaze. For I am the Lord your God, the Holy One of Israel, your Savior." (Isaiah 43:2-3, NIV)

THE FIRE THAT REFINES AND REBUILDS

God's fire doesn't just refine, it also rebuilds.

In ceramics, there's a process called sintering, where intense heat bonds particles together at the atomic level, not by melting them, but by fusing the pieces into something stronger, more solid, and more resilient than before. Isn't that a picture of what God does with our broken pieces? He doesn't throw them away. He takes our shattered pieces, the parts we think are too far gone or broken, and with His gentle, refining touch, He strengthens us. He doesn't let the fire destroy us, He uses it to heal our brokenness and make us into something beautiful and whole.

Initially, I didn't recognize the fire for what it was. I had become so consumed with my pain that my spiritual judgment was clouded. All I knew was that I was drowning and couldn't find my way up for air. Where was God? Why did He feel so distant when I needed Him most?

But He hadn't abandoned me. He was holding me the entire time—guiding me through the fire I thought would break me. I wasn't alone, and I wasn't being destroyed. I was being changed.

Is this where you are right now?

Do you feel like you're barely holding on—like there are too many broken pieces, or you won't survive what you're going through? If so, please hear this: You are in the gentle hands of the Refiner. The hands of the Master Craftsman.

First, God removes. Then, He rebuilds. Right now, you may not see the end of this season. The fire may still feel too intense, the weight too unbearable. But hold on, friend—God is not finished with you yet.

I know this because I've been there. The fire didn't disappear overnight. But something in me began to change. As I stopped resisting and started trusting, the fear began to lose its grip. And in the middle of what should have broken me, I began to feel something I hadn't felt in a long time—peace.

Not the kind of peace that comes when everything's fixed, but the kind that can only come from God.

HEALING STEPS

1. **Acknowledge the Fire.** Take a moment to reflect: What season of refinement have you been walking through? Write down or pray about the challenges you've faced, the emotions that have overwhelmed you, and the questions you've struggled with.

   - Have I resisted God's refining process because of fear or pain? _____

   - Have I mistaken the fire for destruction instead of transformation? _____

   - Where do I feel most broken right now?

   _____

   _____

   _____

   _____

   _____

   _____

   _____

2. **Identify What God is Removing.** God's refining fire isn't meant to destroy you—it's meant to purify and remove what doesn't belong.

   What thoughts, fears, or lies might God be asking me to surrender?

   _____

   _____

_____

_____

_____

_____

_____

Are there areas where I've been trying to hold myself together instead of letting God rebuild me?

_____

_____

_____

_____

_____

_____

What is God burning away so that I can reflect Him more clearly?

_____

_____

_____

_____

_____

_____

"I ... Will refine them as silver is refined, And test them as gold is tested." Zechariah 13:9 (NKJV)

3. **Recognize How God is Rebuilding You**. You are not being left in pieces. God is making you new.

What strength or wisdom have I gained through this refining process?

_____

_____

_____

_____

_____

_____

_____

How has God been present in my pain, even when I didn't see it?

_____

_____

_____

_____

_____

_____

_____

Could it be that God is fusing the broken pieces of my life—like sintering—into something stronger than before?

Where do I see signs of new strength or resilience?

_____

_____

_____

_____

_____

_____

"See, I am doing a new thing! Now it springs up; do you not perceive it?"

Isaiah 43:19 (NIV)

4. **Speak Truth Over Yourself.** What we believe shapes how we heal. The lies we've accepted in the fire must be replaced with truth—God's truth. Speak these aloud. Write them down. Let them take root in your heart.

- **Lie:** "I will never be whole again."
- **Truth:** God is restoring me. He is making all things new. (Revelation 21:5)
- **Lie:** "I am too broken to be used by God."
- **Truth:** His power is made perfect in my weakness. (2 Corinthians 12:9)
- **Lie:** "This fire will destroy me."
- **Truth:** The fire will not consume me. I will come through refined. (Isaiah 43:2, Zechariah 13:9)

SCRIPTURES

- "When you walk through the fire, you will not be burned." Isaiah 43:2-3 (NIV)

- "I ... Will refine them as silver is refined, And test them as gold is tested." Zechariah 13:9 (NKJV)

- "He will sit as a refiner and purifier of silver." Malachi 3:3 (NIV)

- "Do not fear, for I am with you; do not be dismayed, for I am your God." Isaiah 41:10 (NIV)

- "And we know that in all things God works for the good of those who love Him." Romans 8:28 (NIV)

PRAYER PROMPT

Dear Lord,

I come to You as a child in need of her loving Father. I'm struggling, and I'm hurting. I know You haven't abandoned me here, but sometimes, I can't feel You.

Help me, Lord, to not rely on my feelings. I know You are so much more than what I feel at this moment. Your Word tells me You will never leave or forsake me.

I need You, Lord—more than ever before. As this refiner's fire burns, help me to trust Your purpose. Help me to see Your fingerprints wherever I turn. I surrender all to You and ask for Your strength to sustain me, Your wisdom to guide me, Your presence keeps me steady.

Help me to clearly see Your will for my life and the plans You have for me. I long for a deeper relationship with You. Teach me to remain faithful—to You and to Your Word. Let Your Spirit lead me as You will.

Thank You, Lord, for Your goodness and grace. May Your light always shine upon my face. I trust Your purpose. I trust Your plan.

In the sweet name of Jesus,

Amen.

CHAPTER 9
The Gift of Peace

Through this process, something had quietly started to shift inside me. The fire I thought would consume me hadn't gone away—but it didn't feel the same anymore. Somewhere in the middle of the pain, the questions, and the surrender, a quiet strength began to rise. God was doing something I couldn't see yet. And right there, in between what I feared and what I hoped for, I began to feel something I hadn't felt in a long time—peace.

Not the kind of peace that shows up when everything is fixed, but the kind that only God can give—the kind that settles deep in your soul, even when the fire is still burning. That kind of peace is a gift, and it's worth holding onto.

God understands our struggles. He knows the habits, worries, and patterns that try to rob us of the peace He so deeply desires for us. Isaiah 26:3 (NIV) reminds us, "You will keep in perfect peace those whose minds are steadfast, because they trust in you." Peace isn't just given—it must also be guarded.

But remember, this peace isn't something you have to fight for alone. Jesus has already won the battle for your peace. He said, "Peace I leave with you; my peace I give you. I do not give to you as the world gives. Do not let your hearts be troubled and do not be afraid." (John 14:27, NIV)

With God's help, you can begin to let go of the thoughts and habits that pull you away from that peace. When you invite Him into those places and ask Him to reveal what's holding you back, He will renew your mind and transform your heart—little by little.

RECEIVING THE GIFT OF PEACE

Receiving peace can be as simple or as profound as receiving a wrapped gift.

When our son was around seven, he joined a baseball team. After one of his games, we started talking with another family about our faith. That conversation soon led to salvation, and I shared an image that had always helped me understand God's gifts.

I told them it's like receiving a beautifully wrapped present at Christmas. You hold it in your hands, knowing it was chosen just for you—but unless you unwrap it, you'll never experience the joy of what's inside. The gift is already yours, but until you receive it, it remains unopened and unused.

Salvation is the same way. Jesus has already offered us the greatest gift—eternal life. But until we open our hearts to Him, we miss the fullness of what He's done for us.

And peace? It's no different.

Peace is a gift Jesus has already placed in your hands—but it still has to be opened. It's not that the gift isn't real—it's that we haven't accessed what it holds. We begin to unwrap it every time we trust Him with our thoughts, our fears, and the things we can't control. Without that choice, the peace He offers remains a promise—unrealized and unopened.

Overcoming the Peace Robbers

Peace can feel impossible to hold onto when our lives are filled with chaos. Many of us battle what I call "peace robbers"—those quiet but persistent intruders like worry, doubt, and fear. They slip in unnoticed, but once they're there, they stir up anxiety and unrest, clouding our hearts and minds.

Often, these emotions trigger an almost automatic need for control—the belief that if we can manage everything perfectly, maybe we can stop the storm. For me, the urge to fix things has been one of my most stubborn peace robbers. It sneaks in under the disguise of responsibility, but underneath it is fear—fear that if I don't hold everything together, it will all fall apart.

I've laid awake in the early hours, overthinking conversations, trying to solve problems I was never meant to figure out. But all that striving left me weary—mentally, physically, and spiritually. I wasn't protecting peace; I was clinging to control.

Time and time again, God has brought me back to surrender. Not as a one-time decision, but as a daily practice. Trusting Him even when things don't unfold the way I hoped. Trusting that He sees the bigger picture that I can't.

"Trust in the Lord with all your heart, And lean not on your own understanding; In all your ways acknowledge Him, And He shall direct your paths." Proverbs 3:5–6 (NKJV)

These words steady me when my thoughts race and my fears rise. I may not understand the twists and turns of my journey, but I know there's a greater purpose at work—one that's far beyond what I can see.

Using the Burden Balloon to Protect Your Peace

In an earlier chapter, I shared how I picture my fears, sadness and worries being placed in a balloon I call the Burden Balloon. That image has stayed with me, not just as a one-time revelation but as a daily invitation.

Every day, I find myself holding something—some worry, fear, or weight I was never meant to carry. And every day, God gently invites me to release it. To open my hands. To trust Him again.

When I feel anxiety rising or peace slipping away, I pause and ask myself:

- What am I holding onto that's robbing my peace?
- Am I willing to release it into God's hands today?

I'm still learning this—still catching myself trying to fix, control what isn't mine. But when I recognize it, I picture that balloon in my hands, and I let it go. I imagine it rising—lighter, freer—as God takes it from me.

"Do not be anxious about anything, but in every situation, by prayer and petition, with thanksgiving, present your requests to God. And the peace of God, which transcends all understanding, will guard your hearts and your minds in Christ Jesus." (Philippians 4:6–7, NIV)

Peace doesn't come from control—it comes from surrender. And sometimes the greatest act of faith is choosing to let go again today.

A Daily Choice: Guarding Your Peace

Releasing our burdens is one part of protecting peace. But peace also grows through the daily connection through our relationship with Jesus. That's why learning to walk in peace—day after day—is a choice. A *daily* choice. Walking with Jesus means choosing daily surrender—letting go of control, pride, and anything else that keeps us from fully living in His peace.

Another way we guard that peace is by nurturing a consistent relationship with Him Just like we care for our physical health our spiritual health needs daily attention too Spending time with God each day—through prayer Scripture or simply being still in His presence—keeps our hearts anchored when the world feels unsteady.

I've learned this the hard way. When I neglect quiet time with Jesus, it doesn't take long for my peace to start unraveling. My thoughts become scattered. My worries grow louder. My heart drifts. But when I reconnect with Him, even briefly, I feel the change. It's not about checking a box—it's about keeping my soul in rhythm with His.

Peace isn't something we earn. It isn't something we hustle for. It's a gift from Jesus. But like any gift, it can be forgotten, neglected, or pushed aside when life gets overwhelming. Earlier in this chapter, we talked about receiving peace—but living in peace is something different. It's not just a one-time opening; it's a daily choice to keep that gift close, to guard it from the noise, the distractions, and the pull to go back to old patterns.

And here's what I've found: the peace of Jesus isn't fragile. It's not a bubble that pops with one wrong step. It's strong. Unshakable. Rooted in His faithfulness, not my performance.

So today, will you choose to protect the peace He's already given you? Will you let go of what you've been holding too tightly and trust Him again?

"And let the peace that comes from Christ rule in your hearts. For as members of one body you are called to live in peace. And always be thankful." (Colossians 3:15)

As I began to walk in that peace more consistently, I noticed something unexpected. My spirit was calmer, yes—but my body still felt worn out, and my thoughts often scattered. It was like I had received peace in one area, but the others were still struggling to catch up. That's when God began to gently show me: true peace touches every part of who we are—mind, body, and spirit. Peace wasn't lacking—it was leading.

It was the gift that began to restore what had been divided inside me. And that's when God began to show me the bigger picture: I wasn't just created for peace—I was designed for balance.

SCRIPTURES

- "I am leaving you with a gift—peace of mind and heart. And the peace I give is a gift the world cannot give. So don't be troubled or afraid." John 14:27

- "Don't worry about anything; instead, pray about everything. Tell God what you need, and thank him for all he has done. Then you will experience God's peace, which exceeds anything we can understand. His peace will guard your hearts and minds as you live in Christ Jesus." Philippians 4:6-7

- "The Lord gives his people strength. The Lord blesses them with peace." Psalm 29:11

PRAYER PROMPT

Dear Jesus,

Give me the strength to release all of my hurts to You. I don't want to carry these burdens any longer. Protect my mind from the whispers of the enemy—those lies that try to convince me that peace is out of reach, that I must hold onto control, or that the wounds of my past still define me.

When fear and depression rises, remind me that Your peace is stronger. When I am tempted to pick up my burdens again, help me to release them in my Burden Balloon, trusting that You will carry what I cannot. Fill me with a peace that surpasses all understanding, a peace that is not dependent on my circumstances but is anchored in who You are.

I choose to trust You, to surrender control, and to rest in Your perfect peace.

In Jesus' name,

Amen.

CHAPTER 10
Designed for Balance

In the past, I hadn't really thought about how closely connected every part of me was—mind, body, and spirit—until God began to show me that peace wasn't meant to stay in one area. He wanted to restore wholeness. I had been living fragmented, trying to find rest in one part of my life while the others lagged behind. But God had something better in mind: balance.

I poured so much effort into my physical health, thinking that if I could just feel better in my body, everything else would fall into place. But no matter how strong I became on the outside, I still felt spiritually dry and emotionally worn thin.

I didn't get there quickly. But eventually, I reached a place where God could open my eyes—not just to how exhausted I was but to what that exhaustion was really trying to tell me. He showed me that I had been treating symptoms without addressing the deeper need: restoration and alignment. Healing wouldn't come from fixing one area; it had to begin with surrendering every part of myself.

FINDING BALANCE

After God revealed the importance of alignment, He began to show me more about how each part of us—mind, body, and spirit—has different needs. And when one is neglected, the others inevitably suffer.

If we don't care for our physical health, we may lack the strength or stamina to carry out what God has called us to do. If we ignore our spiritual life, we can start to feel distant from God's presence and promises. And if we neglect our minds, we become vulnerable to fear, confusion, and lies that distort the truth of who we are. True health is not just about tending to one part—it's about living in alignment with God's design, so we are fully equipped to reflect His light in the world.

GOD'S BLUEPRINT FOR WHOLENESS

1 Thessalonians 5:23 says, "Now may the God of peace make you holy in every way, and may your whole spirit and soul and body be kept blameless until our Lord Jesus Christ comes again."

This verse doesn't say, "Fix your body and everything else will fall into place." It speaks of wholeness—spirit, soul, and body working together the way God intended. In this context, the soul is what we might call the mind and emotions—the inner life that holds our thoughts, desires, and decisions.

Even elite athletes know that physical strength alone isn't enough. They need mental endurance, emotional resilience, and internal balance. What I was missing wasn't more effort—it was alignment. God wasn't asking me to push harder. He was inviting me to be restored from the inside out.

Most importantly, I began to pray for God to renew my thoughts and break any strongholds that had taken root in my thinking. I prayed for His discernment on what else I needed to do.

In this process, I also learned to extend that same compassion to myself. For so long, I had been harsh with my own heart, measuring my worth by my struggles instead of by His love. But God's renewal wasn't just about removing the darkness; it was about filling my mind with truth, with grace. He was teaching me to think differently—to align my thoughts with His, to reject condemnation, and to replace fear with trust.

Renewal is not just a shift in thinking; it's a revelation of God's heart. When He transforms our minds, He invites us to see as He sees, to love as He loves—even when that love must first be extended inward. And as I embraced His compassion for me, I found I could extend it to others more freely. The kindness I once withheld from myself became a gift I could offer, no longer from a place of emptiness, but from the abundance of His grace.

BODY: A TEMPLE, NOT AN IDOL

Just as God calls us to renew our minds, He also calls us to honor the bodies He's given us. Our bodies aren't meant to be worshipped, but they are meant to be cared for. They allow us to show up—to love, to serve, and to walk out what He's called us to do.

When I started my healing journey, I naturally focused on my physical health first. I was drained and worn out, so it made sense to start there. I tried exercising more, eating better, and getting rest. But God showed me that what I was facing ran deeper than physical exhaustion. My body was tired, yes—but so were my thoughts. My soul felt heavy, and my spirit felt distant. Healthy habits could support me on the outside, but they couldn't touch the broken places inside. Only God could do that.

1 Corinthians 6:19–20 says, "Don't you realize that your body is the temple of the Holy Spirit, who lives in you and was given to you by God? You do not belong to yourself, for God bought you

with a high price. So you must honor God with your body."

That scripture reminded me—my worth wasn't found in how fit or disciplined I could become. I wasn't called to perfect myself. I was called to trust Him. To surrender. God wasn't just asking me to treat my body better—He was asking me to hand over control of every part of me, including the parts I thought I could manage on my own.

Caring for my body still matters, but it was never meant to take the place of the deeper healing God wanted to do. As I surrendered more, I began to see how peace and healing could reach all the way in—from the inside out.

WHAT WE THINK SHAPES US

During that difficult season in my life, I believed a lot of lies—about my worth, my abilities, and my purpose. I was actively working on my body, hoping that would fix everything. But internally, my mind was still tangled in anxiety, depression, and self-doubt. Even as my body grew stronger, my thoughts remained chained.

What we think shapes how we live. When we dwell on fear, negativity, or lies, our choices begin to reflect that internal storm. The enemy loves to sow doubt, and I had unknowingly allowed his whispers to take root. I realized I couldn't trust my thoughts as they were—I needed to renew my mind with God's truth.

His Word was the only thing powerful enough to break the strongholds that had quietly formed in my thinking.

Romans 12:2 (NIV) says, "Be transformed by the renewing of your mind." That verse became an anchor as I learned to surrender my thoughts to Him—not just once, but daily.

Renewing my mind didn't happen by accident. I had to be intentional. It wasn't enough to hope my thoughts would change—I had to actively replace the lies with truth. Every day, I began to speak Scripture over myself, reminding my heart of what God had already said.

And slowly, I began to feel the weight lifting. His mercy wasn't just a concept—it was real. It met me in my brokenness, gently calling me out of despair and into His peace.

As God gently reshaped my thought life, I realized it wasn't just about inner beliefs—it was also about what I allowed to influence me from the outside.

I started asking hard questions:

Is this lifting me up or dragging me down?

Is what I'm watching or listening to reinforcing fear—or strengthening my faith?

What I consumed was shaping how I felt, and what I believed was shaping how I lived.

Friend, have you struggled with this too? Maybe for you it's endless scrolling on social media. Maybe it's the voice of comparison, the steady drip of doubt, or a quiet fear that never fully fades. You try to push past it—staying busy, staying productive, trying to think positive—but it lingers.

You're not alone in that feeling. Many of us live caught between the desire for peace and the pressure to manage it all ourselves. But here's the truth: change starts by paying attention to what we're feeding our thoughts.

What you believe, you live. And if your thoughts are filled with pressure, perfectionism, or fear, your inner world will reflect that unrest. True healing doesn't begin with more doing. It begins with surrender.

SURRENDERING ALL THREE TO GOD

Psalm 46:10 (NKJV) says, "Be still, and know that I am God." That's where true healing begins—with stillness and surrender. Stillness is not a weakness—it's where clarity takes root. It's choosing to open your heart and invite God into the spaces you've tried to control on your own.

For years, I tried to create peace by staying ahead of the chaos. I checked all the right boxes: eating well, journaling, praying, speaking affirmations, attending church. But I was still anxious. I was still tired. That gap between my effort and my peace only grew wider.

It wasn't until I stopped compartmentalizing my healing— my thoughts in one corner, my body in another, and my spirit somewhere in between—that I found real rest. When I finally laid it all before God—without holding back a single piece—things began to change.

Surrender isn't giving up. It's giving *over*. It's releasing what we were never designed to carry in our own strength. It's trusting that God's wisdom is greater than our best strategies. And when we trust Him fully, we stop striving for balance and start living in alignment.

Balance isn't a fixed state—it's a relationship of trust. It's saying, *"God, I give You every part of me—even the parts I don't know how to repair."* When I made that shift, His peace reached places my effort couldn't touch. My soul exhaled. The healing I had been chasing finally started to unfold—not because I earned it but because I stopped resisting it.

FOUNDATION OF TRUE WHOLENESS

I kept doing what I thought was right—making healthy choices, staying productive, trying to stay spiritually grounded. But

I was still anxious. Still tired. The harder I worked to find peace, the more distant it felt. I was unintentionally tending to certain areas of my life while quietly ignoring others, hoping it would be enough.

But real peace didn't come until I brought my whole self to God—my thoughts, my emotions, my physical exhaustion, and even the parts I didn't know how to name. I stopped dividing up what needed healing and finally let Him into all of it.

Surrender isn't giving up—it's handing over what we were never meant to carry alone. It's trusting that God knows how to bring healing in ways we never could. When we release control, we stop chasing balance and start walking in step with Him.

Balance isn't something we master—it's something we learn to trust. It's saying, *"God, here's all of me. Take every part."* And when I finally did that—fully and honestly—I began to feel the steady peace returning—the kind I had once known but had lost beneath the weight of fear, depression, and exhaustion.

It was a steady and consistent peace—not because life got easier but because surrendering more of myself made space for His peace to reside. I was finally accessing the full gift of peace that Jesus offers—not just a moment of calm but a sustaining presence that filled the places I had once tried to manage on my own.

This peace wasn't dependent on circumstances or effort. It reached deeper. It didn't just calm my emotions—it quieted my soul and brought my whole being into alignment with Him. It wasn't about doing more or feeling more in control. It was about being known, held, and led by God in every part of my life.

That's when I realized the imbalance I was feeling wasn't from failure—it came from being disconnected from how God designed me. I wasn't created to live in pieces. I was meant to be whole.

Wholeness isn't about perfection. It's about integration—

letting your mind, body, and spirit move together in step with the One who created them. God doesn't just want to heal a part of you—He wants to make you whole.

As I surrendered my whole self—every thought, every fear, every physical burden—His peace began to touch every part of my life. And the more I aligned with His design, the more I could feel that peace settle in. Not only was He restoring me—He was preparing me to carry that healing into the lives of others.

HEALING STEPS

God didn't create us to live in constant exhaustion, stress, or imbalance. Healing begins when we recognize where we are out of alignment and surrender every part of ourselves—mind, body, and spirit—to Him. Take a moment to reflect on these questions:

1. **Mind Check: Are you filling your mind with God's truth, or have fear, negativity, and unhealthy thought patterns taken over?** Are you filling your mind with God's truth, or have fear, negativity, and unhealthy thought patterns taken over? What we consume—through social media, entertainment, and even our own self-talk—shapes how we think and live.

   _____

   _____

   _____

   _____

   _____

   _____

2. **Body Awareness: Are you caring for your body like a temple of the Holy Spirit or have you been neglecting it?** God calls us to honor our bodies but never to worship them.

_____

_____

_____

_____

_____

_____

_____

"Your body is the temple of the Holy Spirit ... honor God with your body."

1 Corinthians 6:19-20

3. **Spiritual Foundation: Am I seeking God first in all areas of my life?**

"Seek the Kingdom of God above all else, and live righteously, and he will give you everything you need." Matthew 6:33

4. **Identify the Imbalance: Which of the three have I neglected the most and a step I can take this week to bring that area back in balance?**

_____

_____

_____

_____

_____

_____

_____

5. **Surrender & Trust: Have you been trying to "fix" everything in your own strength?**

_____

_____

_____

_____

_____

_____

_____

SCRIPTURES

WHOLENESS & BALANCE

God's Word reminds us that He is the source of our strength, peace, and balance. As you reflect on this chapter, take time to meditate on these Scriptures:

- "A false balance is an abomination to the Lord, but a just weight is His delight." Proverbs 11:1 (ESV)

- "May your whole spirit, soul and body be kept blameless at the coming of our Lord Jesus Christ." 1 Thessalonians 5:23 (NIV)

- "He gives power to the weak and strength to the powerless.

Even youths will become weak and tired, and young men will fall in exhaustion. But those who trust in the Lord will find new strength. They will soar high on wings like eagles. They will run and not grow weary. They will walk and not faint." Isaiah 40:29–31

- "And whatever you do or say, do it as a representative of the Lord Jesus, giving thanks through Him to God the Father." Colossians 3:17

- "It is useless for you to work so hard from early morning until late at night, anxiously working for food to eat; for God gives rest to His loved ones." Psalm 127:2

PRAYER PROMPT

Dear Lord,

Forgive me for allowing myself to become unbalanced. I ask for Your wisdom and discernment to recognize when I'm starting to stray out of alignment from your will.

I thank You for Your loving kindness in guiding me back to wholeness. My heart is full when I think of Your faithfulness, mercy, and grace. I thank You that You never left my side during this difficult journey. I pray Your guiding hand continues to lead me in Your ways so that my life brings You glory. Help me, Lord, to walk in Ephesians 5:8: "For once you were full of darkness, but now you have light from the Lord. So live as people of light!"

In Jesus' name,

Amen.

CHAPTER 11
Share Your Light

You've been through a battle, one that has tested your strength, faith, and endurance. The journey has been gut-wrenching, revealing, and difficult. I'm sure there were moments when you felt exhausted. When you wanted to give up and to stop pushing forward.

I get it, I really do. So before anything else, let me acknowledge how far you've come.

Whether you feel victorious today or still find yourself wrestling with the weight of your burdens, the fact that you're here means you haven't given up. You have kept fighting, kept seeking, kept hoping. And that, my friend, is a victory in itself.

You have begun to see the Light in the darkness, the ray of hope He offers as He pulls you out of despair. The lies of the enemy are being exposed, and you are beginning to recognize how your perception of yourself and your circumstances has been shaped by your past and the battles you've fought.

No longer are you looking through the distorted lenses of the world or the enemy's deceit but through the loving eyes of God, who sees you, cherishes you, and knows your every struggle.

He loves you so much that He has memorized every detail of you, every scar, every tear, every whispered prayer in the dead of night. Just as you've looked at someone you love with deep affection, God looks upon you with even greater tenderness.

Through Jesus' willingness to give of Himself, He empowers you to overcome. In Him, you are no longer a prisoner of your past, you are free. You are no longer defined by your pain, you are redeemed.

Isaiah 42:13 tells us, "The Lord will march forth like a mighty hero; he will come out like a warrior, full of fury. He will shout his battle cry and crush all his enemies." Picture that for a moment: the Lord Himself stepping onto the battlefield for you, defending you, shielding you, fighting off every lie, every fear, every chain that tries to pull you back. You are not alone in this fight. He is your Champion.

From Surviving To Thriving

For so long, maybe you've been stuck in survival mode. Just getting through the day, pushing through the motions, exhausted from carrying more than you were ever meant to. But hear me— God never intended for you to just survive.

He calls you to thrive. He strengthens you not just to endure the storm but to rise above it. He renews your mind so that you can see yourself the way He sees you. Romans 12:2 reminds us, "Let God transform you into a new person by changing the way you think."

Thriving is about more than just making it through the next day. It's about healing, growing stronger, walking in freedom, and deepening your relationship with Him.

A Turning Point: Letting Go of My Burden Balloon

I know this because I've lived it. I remember sitting in the Jeep, that moment I shared with you in chapter 6. It was one of the darkest moments of my life. I felt like I had lost myself in the darkness and couldn't find my way back. My heart was burdened, my spirit fractured, and every attempt to claw my way out had failed.

Even now, that memory brings tears to my eyes because I remember how desperate I felt. But looking back, I also see it as a moment of grace—the moment I finally realized I couldn't fix myself. I needed Jesus.

It was then that I finally began the process of letting go of my Burden Balloon—the weight I had carried for so long. I had been dragging it behind me, afraid to release it, afraid of what would happen if I let go. But God, in His gentleness, showed me that true healing could only begin when I stopped holding on and started trusting Him.

At that moment in the Jeep, I didn't yet know how to surrender completely. I just knew that my way wasn't working anymore. What I didn't realize then was that God was leading me to a deeper breakthrough.

The following weekend, as I knelt at the altar, the weight of it all came crashing down. It was there, in God's presence, that I finally understood. Through the tears, I whispered: *"Help me Jesus, I can't do this anymore. Jesus, help me."* Something shifted. The battle wasn't instantly over, but in that moment, the chains began to break.

Proverbs 3:5-6 became my foundation: "Trust in the Lord with all your heart; do not depend on your own understanding. Seek His will in all you do, and He will show you which path to take."

What once seemed like a moment of despair, I now see as a moment of grace. If I could reach back through time to that broken, hurting girl sitting in the Jeep, I would pull her close, letting her tears soak into my shoulder. I would whisper that she doesn't have to try and carry it all alone. And if you, right now, are in that place, overwhelmed, weary, or unsure if you can keep going, let me speak these same words over you. Let me take your hand, meet your tired eyes, and remind you: Release your burdens to God. He sees you. He hears you. He loves you. This pain will not last forever and you are not alone. Just hold onto Jesus—He's holding onto you.

Your Story Lights Up the Darkness

If you still find yourself in the battle, sweet friend, take heart—your story isn't over. You are seen (Genesis 16:13). You are wanted (Jeremiah 31:3). You are deeply loved (Romans 8:38–39). I know this not just because I believe it, but because God's Word says it's true. So even if you feel weary or unfinished, know this: you are not alone, and you don't have to be "through it" to shine a light for someone else.

Revelation 12:11 says, "And they have defeated him by the blood of the Lamb and by their testimony." Your testimony is powerful. When you share what Jesus has done for you, you are lighting up the darkness for someone else. Because light always spreads. One candle alone may not light an entire room—but together, many flames can drive out the darkness.

When you speak of how Jesus brought you through the storm, you're doing more than telling your story—you're declaring victory over the enemy's lies. You're opening the door for others to step into freedom. Your testimony carries the presence and power of Jesus Himself, and when you share it, His light breaks through again—one heart at a time.

You may not feel ready. You may still be healing. But don't

underestimate how powerful your story already is. God doesn't wait for us to be perfect to use us—He works through our process. And as you share what He's done, you're not just helping someone else begin their healing—you're allowing God to deepen His work in you. Sharing your story invites healing to keep flowing—through you and around you.

Take a quiet moment to ask God: *Where have You already brought light into my life? What part of my story could bring hope to someone else? Who might need the light You've placed in me?*

The light in you has purpose—don't hide it.
Share your light. It matters more than you know.
Let your life light up the darkness!

PRAYER PROMPT

STEPPING INTO THE LIGHT

Heavenly Father,

Thank You for walking with me through this journey. Thank You for healing, restoring, and strengthening me—even in the moments when I couldn't see it happening. I know my story is still being written, and I trust You with every chapter ahead.

Lord, as I continue to walk forward, help me to live boldly in Your light. Fill me with courage to share my testimony so that others may find hope in You. Let my words, my actions, and my love reflect who You are.

I plead the blood of Jesus over my mind, my body, and spirit. Protect me from the lies of the enemy that would try to silence my story or pull me back into fear. Strengthen my spirit so that I can stand firm in the truth of who You say I am.

Jesus, help me to be a light in the darkness. Not because of anything I have done, but because of who You are in me.

I surrender every step ahead to You. Use me, Lord, for Your glory.

In Jesus' name,

Amen.

"You are the light of the world—like a city on a hilltop that cannot be hidden. No one lights a lamp and then puts it under a basket. Instead, a lamp is placed on a stand, where it gives light to everyone in the house. In the same way, let your good deeds shine out for all to see, so that everyone will praise your heavenly Father." Matthew 5:14-16

STEPPING INTO THE LIGHT: PERSONAL PROMPTS

You've read stories of healing. You've been reminded of the truth. Now, take a few quiet moments to reflect on what God is doing in your own life.

There's no pressure to have it all figured out. This isn't about being ready or perfect. It's about being honest. Open. Willing. Just as you are.

Use the prompts below as a guide—not a checklist. Let the Holy Spirit speak as you write, reflect, or simply sit with the questions in your heart.

Use the space below or your own journal. This is your story, your healing, your moment to step into the light.

1. **Where have I seen God bring light into my life—even in dark or painful places?**

   _____

   _____

   _____

   _____

   _____

   _____

   _____

2. **What part of my story could bring hope to someone else?**

   _____

   _____

   _____

   _____

_____

_____

_____

3. What lies has the enemy tried to speak over me that I
   now reject in Jesus' name?

_____

_____

_____

_____

_____

_____

4. How has God's healing in my life made me more compas-
   sionate, humble, or aware of others?

_____

_____

_____

_____

_____

_____

5. Who is one person—or one space—where I can begin to share light and hope when I feel led?

_____

_____

_____

_____

_____

_____

_____

Epilogue

You don't have to be fully healed to begin walking in the light. We are all a work in progress. You just have to keep walking.

If you've made it to this final page, I want to thank you for allowing me to come alongside you on this journey. Take a moment to pause and recognize just how far you've come. You've chosen honesty over hiding and faced some painful places in your story. You've opened your heart to truth, even when it was hard.

That's no small thing—and it's not just personal growth. That's spiritual courage and surrender. And that, my friend, is the beginning of freedom.

Remember the Burden Balloon? It's held more than just thoughts—it's carried your fears, your tension, and the quiet pain you never expected to hold so long. And maybe now, it's grown heavier than you realized. But you don't have to keep carrying it. Let it go—gently, again and again, until you feel the burden lighten. Every time you release something to God, you make room for God's light to shine brighter in you.

You may not feel like a beacon yet, but light doesn't need to be glaring to make a difference. Even the smallest flame can chase away the dark. Keep leaning into Jesus. Keep inviting Him into your story. And as His light begins to steady and strengthen in you, don't be surprised when it starts to shine through you—at exactly the moment someone else needs to see it.

"The Lord is my strength and my shield;

my heart trusts in Him, and He helps me.

My heart leaps for joy, and with my song I praise Him."

Psalm 28:7

"The light shines in the darkness, and the darkness can never extinguish it."

John 1:5

Resources

Analogy References

Throughout this book, I've used visual metaphors to help illustrate the emotional and spiritual journey of healing, surrender, and transformation. Some are personal images God placed on my heart, and others are inspired by real-world concepts that reflect deeper spiritual truths.

The Burden Balloon (Personal Analogy):

The Burden Balloon is a visual image God gave me to illustrate how we often carry the weight of our fears, worries, and responsibilities. As we hold onto these burdens, the pressure builds. But like a balloon, our hearts weren't meant to stretch endlessly under pressure—we're meant to release those burdens to God. This picture helps us understand surrender not as giving up but as handing over what we were never meant to carry.

The Funhouse Mirror (Personal Analogy):

The Funhouse Mirror is a metaphor God used to help me understand how fear and depression distort our perception. Just like a carnival mirror twists our physical reflection—making parts of us appear exaggerated, missing, or unrecognizable—emotional struggles can warp the way we see ourselves and the world. This analogy reminds us that our feelings aren't always the truth, and that only God's Word reflects who we truly are.

Sintering (Ceramics/Materials Science Concept):

Sintering is a high-heat process used to bond ceramic particles together without melting them. It strengthens and solidifies the material, making it more durable. This process serves as a powerful metaphor for how God uses life's refining fire—not to destroy us, but to strengthen and transform us from the inside out.

Adapted in part from *Sintering: Theory and Practice* by Randall M. German

Mental Health Resources

If you or someone you love is struggling with depression, anxiety, or suicidal thoughts, please reach out. Help is available, and you are not alone.

National Institute of Mental Health

- Mental Health Information
  https://www.nimh.nih.gov/health/topics/mental-health-information

NIMH Health Topics Overview

- Health Topics. U.S. Department of Health and Human Services.
  https://www.nimh.nih.gov/health/topics

Crisis Support & Hotlines
National Suicide & Crisis Lifeline (US):

- Dial **988** anytime for 24/7, free and confidential support. Visit: https://988lifeline.org

Crisis Text Line:

- Text **HOME** to **741741** (available in the U.S. and Canada) to connect with a trained crisis counselor.

RAINN (Rape, Abuse & Incest National Network):

- For survivors of sexual violence seeking confidential support.
- Call **1-800-656-4673** or visit: https://www.rainn.org

SAMHSA National Helpline:

- For mental health and substance use treatment referrals.
- Call **1-800-662-HELP (4357)** or visit: https://www.samhsa.gov